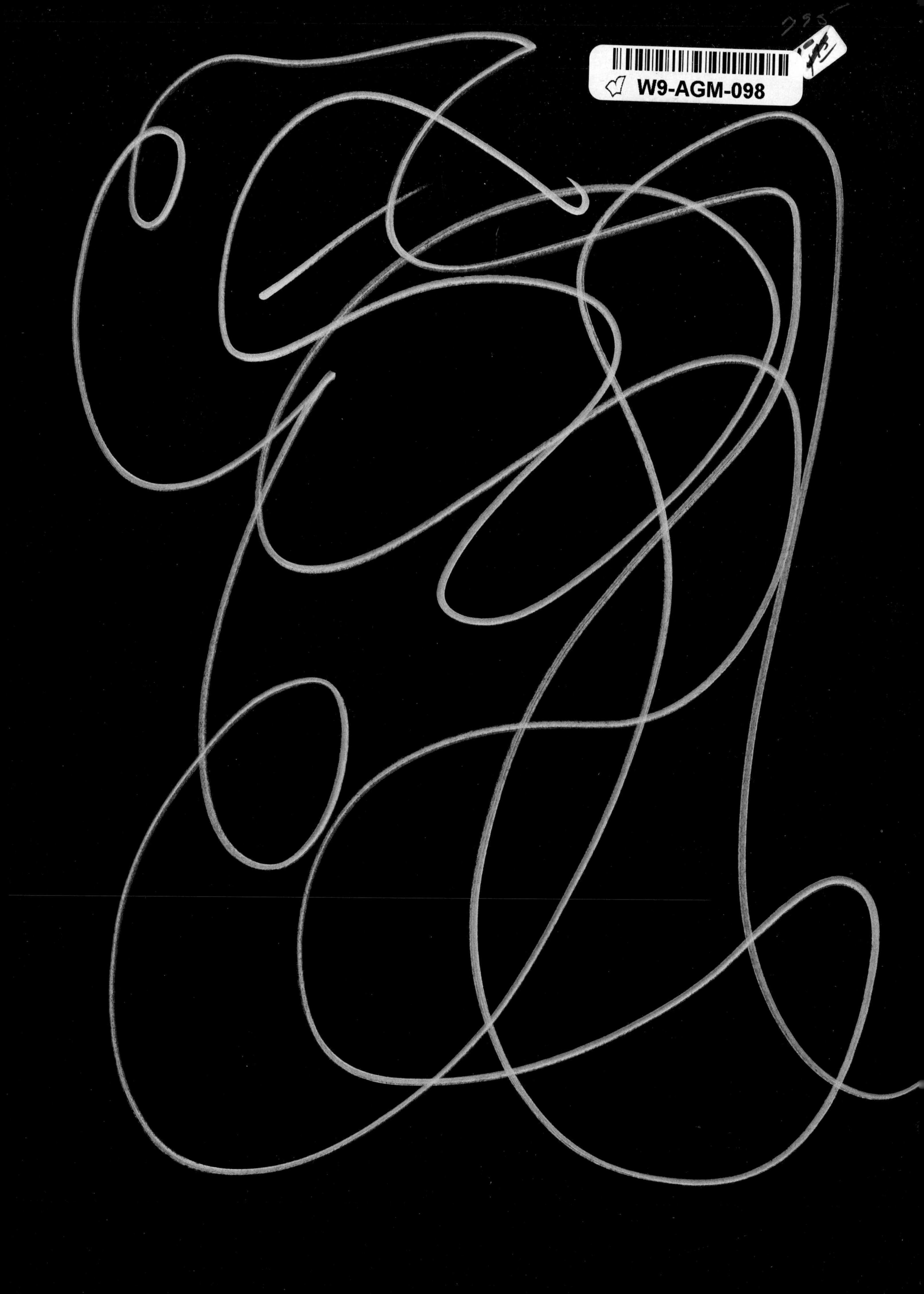

MAN THROUGH HIS ART **MUSIC**

OTHER VOLUMES

TO BE PUBLISHED ARE:

Man and Animal

The Human Face

The Family

Festivals

Nature

Man at Work

Charity

The Vision of Bliss

Death

Dreams and Fantasy

The Experience of God

Love and Marriage

ALREADY IN PRINT:

War and Peace

Man through his Art

VOLUME 2

MUSIC

PUBLISHED IN THE UNITED STATES WITH THE SPONSORSHIP OF THE

World Confederation of Organizations of the Teaching Profession (WCOTP)

and with the Financial Help of UNESCO.

New York Graphic Society

Greenwich, Connecticut

FIRST EDITION 1964

First published in the United Kingdom by
EDUCATIONAL PRODUCTIONS LIMITED, 17 Denbigh Street, London SW I

Made and printed in Great Britain

General Preface

Nowhere is the record of man's social progress through the ages portrayed more vividly than in his art: It is a profound experience to study the great masterpieces of artistic expression and to see how the artist has captured for all time the many facets of man's character. We gain a deeper insight into man as he is from seeing man as he was.

The World Confederation of Organizations of the Teaching Profession has been pleased to sponsor *Man Through His Art* in the belief that the educational material thereby made available will constitute a valuable aid in the hands of teachers everywhere in furthering mutual appreciation of Eastern and Western cultural values. The editorial responsibility for the text and illustrations lies with the Editors, Madame Anil de Silva and Professor Otto von Simson, whose inspiration and creative efforts have made possible the promotion of the project.

William G. Carr

SECRETARY-GENERAL

World Confederation
of Organizations
of the Teaching Profession

THIS VOLUME

This second volume of MAN THROUGH HIS ART illustrates, with carefully selected masterpieces of the visual arts accompanied by authoritative commentaries, the profound part played by Music in the life of Man throughout historical times. Inevitably the great visual artists have been aware of the significant rôle of Music, have been inspired by their sister art, and have chosen it as a theme of some of their greatest and most moving works. The masterpieces illustrated and discussed in this Volume, which range in time from an early Egyptian relief to Nicolas de Staël's contemporary *Musicians,* have been chosen to illustrate the continuity of the theme and the variety of its meaning to Man in different cultures and civilizations.

Mere representations of musicians or musical performances as such have not been chosen, although inevitably the participants – the players and the listeners – are generally present; but rather, examples are chosen in which the visual arts most "aspire to the condition of music." For example, the representation of Lausanne Cathedral illustrates that consonance between musical harmony and visual harmony, which has prompted the description of architecture as "frozen music"; and at the same time this masterpiece conveys through an architectural composition the "symphony of all creation." With the Anthropomorphic Harp, of distant origin, but still played in parts of Africa, it is the carving of the musical instrument itself which expresses "something of the mood and spirit of the player and anticipates something of the music he will produce." In spanning the wide range in Time and Place this volume illustrates and discusses, among other masterpieces of the visual arts, such diverse works as the early Egyptian relief of the *Blind Harpist* and a Greek vase painting depicting the ecstatic music of Dionysus; carvings and wall paintings from India and Java; a Pre-Colombian Mexican fresco; a panel by Fra Angelico; Grünewald's *Mystic Birth,* with its strange and intense rapture, expressing as music "Man's response to ultimate reality"; the lyrical music of a scroll painting by T'ang Yin and of an oil painting by Giorgione, both of around 1500; an Iranian miniature which helps to illustrate the more specifically Eastern approach to Music; the splendid orchestration of colour of Rembrandt's *David and Saul;* and de Staël's *Musicians,* evoking the pungency of contemporary jazz.

These superb examples of artistic expression are accompanied by informative and authoritative text notes prepared by acknowledged experts on their respective subjects, named as *Contributors* on page 7.

THE SERIES

This series of 14 books has been sponsored by the World Confederation of Organizations of the Teaching Profession with the financial help of UNESCO. It is intended as an aid to international understanding and a contribution to the UNESCO major project for mutual appreciation of Eastern and Western cultural values.

The present volume and the other thirteen in the series will present, describe and annotate artistic masterpieces from every major culture and almost every nation in the world.

Each volume will illustrate a particular theme. These themes have been so selected from the broad range of man's experience that almost every aspect of his everyday life is represented.

Each book contains sixteen plates in full colour and four in black and white. Tremendous care has been taken in the selection and reproduction of these. The editors have tried to insure that the masterpieces chosen present as wide and as varied a survey of each theme as possible.

The Editors are Madame Anil de Silva, author of *The Life of Buddha, Chinese Landscape Painting from the Tun-Haung Caves,* Professor Otto von Simson, author of *The Gothic Cathedral, The Sacred Fortress – Byzantine Art and Statecraft in Ravenna,* etc., Dr. Roger Hinks, author of *A Catalogue of Greek and Roman Paintings and Mosaics in the British Museum, A Handbook of Greek and Roman Portrait Sculpture,* etc., and Philip Troutman, Curator of Courtauld Institute Galleries, London, and author of *El Greco.*

Editors and contributors

EDITORS

Madame Anil de Silva
Professor Otto von Simson
Roger Hinks †
Philip Troutman

ASSOCIATE EDITORS

Professor Rama Prasana Naik,
Joint Secretary, Ministry of Education, Government of India

Professor Soichi Tominaga,
Director of the National Museum of Western Art,
Tokyo, Japan

CONTRIBUTORS

Jacqueline Delange,
Musée de l'Homme, Paris

Dr Gisèle Freund,
author of *Mexique Précolumbien*

Dr Roger Hinks, †
author of *A Catalogue of Greek and Roman Paintings and Mosaics in the British Museum*, *A Handbook of Greek and Roman Portrait Sculpture*, *Carolingian Art*, etc.

Dr Fakhir Hussain,
Fellow, Institut d'Esthétique, Paris
author of *Essays on Literature* and *Essays on Aesthetics* (*trans. into Urdu*)

Madame Lilian Lassen,
Ecole du Louvre, Paris

Srimati Geeta Satyadeva Mayor,
Sitarist,
India

Dr Sita Narasimhan,
Additional Professor of English, Presidency College, Madras
articles on the *Vedas*, etc.

Dr Elizabeth Rosenbaum,
author of *A Catalogue of Cyrenaican Portrait Sculpture*, etc.

Madame Anil de Silva,
author of *The Life of Buddha*
and *Chinese Landscape Painting from the Caves of Tun-Huang*

Professor Otto von Simson,
author of *The Gothic Cathedral*, *The Sacred Fortress – Byzantine Art and Statecraft in Ravenna*, etc.

Professor Michael Sullivan,
author of *The Birth of Landscape Painting in China*

Morikuni Toda,
composer and Permanent Delegate for the Government of Japan with UNESCO

Professor Soichi Tominaga,
Director of the National Museum of Western Art, Tokyo

Philip Troutman,
Curator, Courtauld Institute Galleries, London
author of *El Greco*

Dr Peter C. Ucko,
Department of Anthropology, University of London

Contents

Acknowledgements

THE EDITORS cannot record their thanks individually to all those who have given their disinterested help and encouragement to this project from its inception.

Special thanks are due to the Asia Society, New York, who provided assistance for the preparative work of this project; to the Unesco Secretariat, without whose constant guidance and active assistance this project could not have materialised; and to Mr Harvey Miller of the Phaidon Press, who liberally prepared material and helped the editors with technical advice for over two years.

A debt of appreciation is also acknowledged to the National Commissions for Unesco of Cambodia, the Federal Republic of Germany, France, Great Britain, India, Japan, Mexico, New Zealand, the Sudan, Sweden, Switzerland, the UAR, and the USA, who have given a great deal of help to the project in various ways. The illustrations are reproduced by courtesy of the following museums, private collectors and photographers.

Plate 1 and Fig. 1, the Rijksmuseum van Oudheden, Leiden, Holland. Plate 2, text extracts with acknowledgements to Erwin Rohde, *Psyche;* Plate 2, the Bibliothèque Nationale, Paris; Fig. 2, the Musées-Royaux des Beaux-Arts, Brussels, photograph Copyright A.C.L., Brussels. Plate 3, the Victoria and Albert Museum, London; Figs. 3a, 3b and 3c, photograph by Werner Bischof, Magnum Photos. Plate 4 and Fig. 4, the Musée Guimet, Paris, and the National Museum Service, Versailles. Plate 5, photograph by Gisèle Freund. Plate 6, photograph by Held, Lausanne. Plate 7 and Figs. 7a, 7b and 7c, the National Gallery, London. Plate 8, the National Palace Museums, Taiwan, and with the good offices of the Freer Gallery of Art, Washington; photograph by Henry Beville. Plate 9, the Louvre Museum, Paris; photograph by Scala, Florence. Plate 10 and Figs. 10a to 10f, the Musée d'Unterlinden, Colmar, France; photographs by Phaidon Press Limited. Plate 11, the Imperial Museum, Teheran, photograph by UNESCO; Fig. 11, the British Museum, London. Plate 12, text extract from *The Tale of Genji* (translation by Arthur Waley), reproduced by kind permission of George Allen and Unwin Limited, London; Plate 12 and Fig. 12, the Freer Gallery of Art, Washington. Plate 13, the Louvre Museum, Paris, photograph by Scala, Florence, Fig. 13, Giraudon, Paris. Plate 14, the Mauritshuis, The Hague; Fig. 14, the Städel Institut, Frankfurt/Main. Plate 15, the Victoria and Albert Museum, London. Plate 16, the Smithsonian Institute and the Freer Gallery of Art, Washington. Plate 17, the Museum of Fine Arts, Boston, U.S.A., photograph by Sandak, New York. Plate 18, the Musée Reitberg, Zurich (the von der Heydt collection), photograph by Zoe Binswanger, Zurich; Fig. 18a, Musée de l'Homme, Paris; Fig. 18b, Eric Dampierre. Plate 19, by courtesy of the artist and the Musée d'Art Moderne, Paris, all rights reserved by A.D.A.G.D., 1963, Paris, photograph by Scala, Florence. Plate 20, all rights reserved by A.D.A.G.D., 1963, Paris; photograph by Editions Georges Fall, Paris.

The man that hath no music in himself,
Nor is not moved with concord of sweet sounds,
Is fit for treasons, stratagems and spoils;
The motions of his spirit are dull as night,
And his affections dark as Erebus:
Let no such man be trusted . . .

Shakespeare, *Merchant of Venice*, Act V, Scene I

When the people dance and sing
and play on their several musical instruments,
they make the Deity happier
than by their Meditational practices –
thus have we heard

JAIMINIYA, 12, 22

Introduction

THE DISTINCTION in kind between music and the visual arts – the one art existing in time, the other in space – is a fundamental one. You cannot play music or read poetry backwards, and make sense. Whereas it is indifferent whether you begin to examine a building inside or outside; or whether you look at the front of a statue first, or the back; or whether you start looking at a picture from the top right hand corner or the bottom left: the examination of the whole will take some time, but it is the spectator's own time; and the choice of the order of experience is left to him, for he is an active participant in the process of appreciation. But a poem, a play, a symphony have each to be experienced in its proper sequence; and the public has to submit, individuals responding together simultaneously.

In all countries there are probably people who are impatient of this constraint, who claim the right to take in their own impressions in their own time and at their own pace. Such people, perhaps, are by nature refractory to music and poetry and drama; feel at ease only with painting, sculpture and architecture. The reason may be that they are secretly afraid of the passing of time, appalled by the approach of death; they long to be rescued from events by those arts of which time is not a fundamental part – pictures and statues and buildings. Yet a kind of unheard, unhurrying music, echoes unendingly in the background of their minds; and they seek to fix it and point to it in the still but somehow vibrant shapes of certain works of visual art.

For there are musical pictures, just as there are unmusical ones, pictures that are positively hostile to the whole notion of music; and it is the object of this album to select and comment upon precisely this distinguishing element of musicality, and try to exclude (for this particular purpose) the element of non-musicality in the visual imagery of the West and the East alike. Our purpose therefore is to depict the principle of visual harmony akin to music. We are not primarily concerned with representations of music as such, for the task of representing what is audible visually is the task of depicting an art that unfolds in time by the simultaneity of a single impression.

Often enough, the least musical pictures (in our sense) are precisely those in which the persons represented are most busily engaged in 'making' music, or in which musical instruments are most conspicuously displayed. In how many pictures of a musical company do we not feel that the persons involved are (as amateurs) merely displaying a polite accomplishment for the sake of social prestige, or (as professionals) exhibiting their virtuosity to an admiring, and usually a self-admiring, public?

Yet there are, of course, pictures which really do, in Pater's phrase, *aspire to the condition of music:* pictures in which the music is intrinsic, emanates – almost in spite of themselves – from the men and women involved, resounding – as it were – in the very pictorial texture of the piece. Not all pictures of people 'making' music are musically unconvincing: in not a few cases the artist is a sufficiently good psychologist to be able to convey by expression or gesture the rapt and self-forgetful look of those who have really lost themselves in the sounds conjured forth. For it is not difficult to judge whether the musicians are serious or not: whether they are truly absorbed in their playing and singing, or are smirking at the audience.

Or again: there are plenty of truly musical pictures that represent the pauses in the performance rather than its actual movement. In fact, many musicians when they are being painted prefer to be exhibited as tuning up: it exempts them from the obligation to put on an act of concentration for the spectator's benefit; and it creates the atmosphere of suspense, when music has just sounded and is soon to be heard again – that moment which is extended from the rhythm of the music itself to the intervals between the movements. There are indeed persons so musical that they only perfectly enjoy the intermission, because only then can they reflect in tranquility upon the emotion just past, and anticipate confidently the emotion just to come. It is thus that one may interpret some of the most inspired renderings of musical intermissions (for example, Giorgione's *Concert Champêtre*, Plate 9). The music hangs in the air, vibrates in the memory: for some lovers of painting and music, at least, such pictures are the most musical of all.

For pictures of music in action are rarely so suggestive. Painting, after all, is essentially an art of stillness: to bring in the ideal dimension of time, in which music has its being, is to invite disquiet. In seventeenth-century Holland, the music-lesson, with the fumbling beginner and the patient master, is a commoner theme than the assured performance.

The difference between the European and the non-European approach to the relations between sight and sound in the arts is hard for either party to determine. The European may feel, for instance, that the Chinese and the Indians and the Persians (Plates 8, 15, 11) are nearer to him in their visual expression of musical sensibility than, say, the Egyptians, the Africans, or the Pre-Columbian Americans (Plates 1, 18, 5); but he will find it hard to define exactly why this is. It is no doubt when the rhythm is most marked or the element of time most dominant, that music is furthest away from the visual arts, and a visual equivalent most difficult to find. One may witness, as it were, those drummers, harpists and trumpeters playing on their instruments; and one's experience may explain and one's imagination does its best to realise, what those drum-beats, those harp plucks and trumpet blasts sound like. But one cannot fully sympathize, or empathize, unless the artist has managed to find a visual symbol for the musical effect: by means, for example of brilliant colour to render strident sound. The legendary blind man who felt that scarlet must be like a trumpet-blast lives again in Nicolas de Staël's *The Musicians* (Plate 20), where the flaming reds and yellows juxtaposed with sharp blues do convey with real conviction the pungency of jazz.

Where, on the other hand, melody prevails, the rise and fall of the tune can be suggested in the flow of line; and the musical intervals in the spacing of shapes, on the purest Pythagorean principles. In this sense it is meaningful to describe as 'musical' certain compositions of Gothic and Renaissance architecture which are explicitly based upon the Greek philosopher's relation of number and pitch, and whose proportions may in consequence suggest the static relationship of sound and space (Plate 6). And since colour also can be measured – spectroscopically in terms of wave-lengths – it is not entirely fanciful to detect certain affinities of colour and pitch. More plausible, however, is the contention, often made when analysing the effect of Persian miniatures (Plate 11), that there is a real, if empirical, connexion between the size of a patch of colour and the intensity of its tone and tint; and that melodic sequences may be easily imagined from the arrangement of coloured patches as well as from the movement of the linear pattern. These relations are, no doubt, a matter of personal feeling in the sensitive spectator, and cannot be scientifically demonstrated; but they are not necessarily the less valid for that.

Asian music, being purely melodic and free in rhythm, can be suggested by the flowing, swaying lines of the design, and its tonality may be implied by the chromatic range of the whole composition. Here at least the European is at a disadvantage: he has lost the power to respond emotionally to any modes but the major and the minor, which he still equates with 'cheerful' and 'sad' moods.

On the other hand, the European does respond very readily to the clear and 'singing' colour of a Persian miniature (Plate 11), to the voluptuous movement of an Indian sculptured frieze or fresco (Plates 3, 4), to the rhythmic calligraphy of a Chinese scroll (Plate 8), even if he knows he is missing all the overtones and associations that make them precious to the Asian mind and eye. And he knows that the richness and variety of his own musical and pictorial tradition have been purchased by the sacrifice of purity, clarity and directness. By comparison with the art of Asia his own art has shown a certain evasiveness, a certain tendency to obliqueness in its musical analogies. But when in recent years the European artist has wished to create a permanent image of movement in time, he is forced (like Matisse) to rely upon the intermediate art of the dance, where alone music becomes visible, but whose effect is of its very nature as evanescent as music itself. This is, of course, an agelong resource, in Europe, in India, and elsewhere: in ancient Greece the tragic dance became the tragic drama, and the tragic drama must doubtless have influenced the schemes and compositions of plastic and pictorial art; and so through the Middle Ages and down to modern times. This may be obvious enough. What is less easy to demonstrate is that real sympathy that may exist between a painter and a composer, and it is especially these 'divinations of private congruity' that are here to be explored, this kinship between visual harmony and music.

Roger Hinks †

1. THE BLIND HARPIST
The Rijksmuseum, Leiden, Holland

Painted relief from the Tomb of Pa-aten-em-heb, Saqqara (Memphis), Egypt. *Ca.* 1375-1360 BC.

The Blind Harpist 1

Painted relief. Tomb of Pa-aten-em-heb, Saqqara (Memphis), Egypt. *c.* **1375–1360 BC**

A note on music in ancient Egypt. From scenes painted on the walls of tombs, as well as from the actual objects found during excavations, we can tell that the clapping of hands or sticks gave the rhythm to accompany such things as work in the fields or the pressing of wine. As entertainment for secular or funerary purposes, instruments were

PLATE I is a detail from a painted chalkstone relief from the tomb of Pa-aten-em-heb at Saqqara (Memphis), where it formed the right-hand wall of the tomb.

The whole relief (Fig. I) shows four musicians seated in two rows behind a shaven priest clad in a panther skin, who pours an offering and burns incense before two large and two smaller seated figures representing the deceased, his wife and possibly his two daughters. Inscribed above the group is the song to which the musicians are playing the accompaniment.

Fig. I. *The painted relief from the Tomb of Pa-aten-em-heb, nobleman of the Court of Akhenaten. Saqqara (Memphis), Egypt.*

The relief dates from the Amarna Period (*c.* 1375–60 BC) of the New Kingdom, from the time of King Amenhotep IV (Akhenaten). The artistic freedom and naturalism favoured by Akhenaten is strongly evident in this scene, within the context of the formal treatment of funerary representations of the time. The musical instruments are so carefully represented that the details of their manufacture can easily be made out: the strings of the harp, for instance, can be seen to be made taut by their attachment to the pegs. Although the harpist is represented in the formal posture known from many other representations, the naturalism of such details as, for instance, the hanging stomach and the contracted muscles around his mouth are striking. This figure of the blind player concentrating on his music is portrayed with conviction and sympathy.

From its content and style the song inscribed above the relief (better preserved on a complete papyrus of slightly later date) must date back to the Middle Kingdom (*c.* 2134–1786 BC). The beginning of the song accepts death and the uncertainty of life. Following this comes a change of mood:

And they who built houses – their places are not.
See what has been made of them!
I have heard the words of Ii-em-hotep and Hor-dedef,
With whose discourses men speak so much.
What are their places now?
Their walls are broken apart, and their places are not –
As though they had never been!
And there is no-one who comes back from over there,
That he may tell their state,
That he may tell their needs,
That he may still our hearts,
Until we too may travel to the place where they have gone.

The song ends with the advice to enjoy oneself as much as possible while still on this earth, as everything else is uncertain:

Refrain:
Make holiday, and weary not therein!
Behold, it is not given to a man to take his property with him.
Behold, there is not one who departs who comes back again!

The song is unusual in its pessimism. In the vast majority of funerary representations the musicians and the song are concerned either to console the dead who are about to start their journey to the judgement scene or to 'make holiday' for the dead in their future life. The special circumstances of the time may account for the choice of this song dating from the Middle Kingdom: the First Intermediate Period (*c.* 2258–2140 BC) had also been one of turmoil and doubt, and the reiteration of the song in the New Kingdom may reflect the spiritual questioning of the Amarna Period of King Akhenaten, who had attempted to impose the worship of the one god Aten in place of the many deities worshipped before his time.

Music played an important part in ancient Egypt especially in a funerary context at mortuary feasts to entertain the dead (as in this relief), but also in a secular or domestic context, when a husband would be entertained by music at everyday parties, or music would accompany work in the fields. Musicians were highly esteemed; some were of noble rank, others were professionals. Already in the Old Kingdom (*c.* 2680–2258 BC) a musician was appointed in charge of musical activities at court and the names of individual musicians appear on some reliefs. Our knowledge of the role of music in ancient Egypt depends almost exclusively on the practice of painting, modelling and carving objects and scenes in their tombs, and our acquaintance with the actual instruments employed is further assisted by the dry climate which has preserved so many.

From the time at least of the Middle Kingdom it was a common feature of Egyptian representations of harpists to show them as blind. In ancient Egypt the blind were treated with great consideration and it is perhaps not surprising that they should have been chosen for this most suitable employment. A less happy conjecture is that the frequency of blind musicians was due to the

played either singly, as a small ensemble, or as a larger group or orchestra, with a conductor or leader to indicate entrances or set the rhythm.

In the Old Kingdom (*c.* 2680–2258 BC), the typical Egyptian musical ensemble consisted of a singer, a harpist and flautist, and sometimes a clarinettist. From the New Kingdom onwards (from *c.* 1570 BC), the orchestra included many varieties of harp with numerous strings, and trumpets, lutes, lyres and drums. We can, therefore, deduce that Egyptian music had become progressively louder and more varied; while the dance scenes accompanying New Kingdom representations suggest that the steps had also become more animated.

The majority of clappers were held in one hand only, and were often shaped in the form of the human hand and arm. The sistrum, which consisted of a metal frame with several loosely-fitted cross wires, was shaken to produce the sound. The clarinet was made of two pieces of cane bound together, one probably producing a droning sound, while the other played the tune. Drums were variously round, oval, and rectangular, and were covered on both sides with skins kept taut by thongs. The large lyre was held with the strings away from the performer, with both hands plucking them; while the smaller version was held upright in the arms. The trumpet was originally a military instrument in Egypt; very fine examples were found in the tomb of Tutankhamen (*c.* 1357–1349 BC) of copper, bronze and silver, which could still be played today with the addition of modern mouth-pieces. The harp represented in the present scene is one of many types used in ancient Egypt. In the Old Kingdom harps were small with few strings, whereas later, large ones also were played and the instruments were lavishly decorated and had over twenty-three strings.

P.J.U.

Bibliography

Lange and Hirmer
Egypt
Phaidon Press, London, 1956

For the translation of the song:
Ancient Near East Texts
ed. James B. Pritchard
Princeton, 1955

For the songs of the harpists:
Miriam Lichtheim,
The Songs of the Harpers
Journal of Near Eastern Studies, IV, 1945

For musical instruments:
Curt Sachs
Altägyptische Musikinstrumente
Der Alte Orient, XXI, 1920

For the role of music:
Hans Hickman
45 *Siècles de Musique dans l'Egypte Ancienne*
Paris, 1956

husband's reluctance to allow anyone to come into close contact with the women of the house. It is however not so certain that the blind harpist was still commonly employed at the time this relief was made, and it is possible that the persistence of representations of the blind harpist at this time may have been a stylistic convention divorced from reality. While this may be the case, in this present relief the introduction of the blind harpist is indeed effective. The artist has observed from life and portrayed for us with great understanding this blind player of three-and-a-half thousand years ago.

Peter J. Ucko

2 Dionysus and the dancing Satyrs

Attic Cup by the 'Painter of Brygos', Greece. Beginning of 5th century BC

THE SCENE of this drinking vessel represents the god Dionysus (Bacchus), playing the lyre, his head thrown back in ecstasy, flanked by two dancing satyrs, one with clappers, a kind of castanets, in each hand, the other holding clappers in one hand and a large vine scroll in the other. All three figures are crowned with vine leaves. Dionysus appears to be listening to the music of his lyre: his left hand still fingers the strings, and in his right hand he holds the plectrum which his pose suggests he has just used for playing a particularly stirring rhythmical accompaniment to the tune. Ordinarily, the lyre is connected with lyrical or epic poetry, but it is clear that in this painting its music produces an intense ecstasy in the player and dancers. This ecstatic character of the music and dance so vividly expressed is intrinsic to the meaning of Dionysus, who represents a fundamental part of the Greek spirit as of the human spirit in general.

The god Dionysus is intimately linked with the music, poetry and drama of ancient Greece. To appreciate this link it is necessary to understand the origins of Greek drama and music and the part played in their development by the cult of Dionysus.

Dionysus is one of the most ancient of Greek gods. It was in Thrace, where the cult was of special importance, that the belief in eternal life for the soul first appears, and this belief was integrated into the cult of Dionysus, which thus will have fertilised the first germs of belief in immortality. The idea of immortality was not immediately accepted by the Greeks, who in the early stages of their development elevated only their heroes to this status. True mysticism is fundamentally based on the essential union, realised through religion, of the divine and human spirit, and the rituals of the Dionysian cult helped those taking part to achieve this unity with God by a 'sacred madness' or 'possession', for it was believed that man could not enter into communication with superior beings, or with God, except by the exaltation of his whole being. Every two years the return of Dionysus was celebrated, and the return of the god was the occasion and motive of the ritual whereby the believer could become one with him, for in a state of ecstasy the soul could escape from the body and join in the life of the god.

The part played by music in this ritual was all-important. In Thrace, where the ritual was more violent than in Greece, it was held on a mountain, in the obscurity of night, and in the uncertain, flickering light of torches. A powerful music was made by the beating of great cauldrons of metal, by the clang of heavy cymbals, and above all by the profound call of the notes of the flute which invited one to madness – when the soul was first awakened. Excited by this savage music the participants danced with shrill cries of joy. There was no question of their singing (the singing was generally provided by a chorus) for the dance took away their breath. 'It was not the measured movements executed by the Greeks of Homer when they danced and chanted, but a circular dance, turbulent and furious, plunging those taking part into a sort of ecstasy of madness and obsession. In reality this orgiastic cult is a manifestation seen at all times and in all degrees of civilisation, and must therefore derive its need from the profound physical and psychological depths of man.' (Rohde)

We are told that 'it was the sound of these instruments together with the dance that helped produce the extreme tension necessary for the state of ecstasy by which the spirit was able to merge into the world of the gods. God enters into men . . . In fact the Dionysian cult was only a variant of those practices by which more than half of humanity tries to approach the divine.'

The most sublime expression of poetry and drama had its origins in the

The anonymous painter of the vase, the 'Painter of Brygos', is recognised by a characteristic style of painting which appears on several vases made and signed by the potter Brygos who employed several painters in his workshop. He was the best of these painters, and indeed, one of the greatest draughtsmen in the whole of Greek art.

Professor Chamoux's extensive note on the technique of Greek vase painting appears in *Man Through His Art*, Vol. 1, *War and Peace*, Plate 3.

Greek art in general was indebted to a certain extent to the art of other peoples, such as the Cretans and Egyptians. In sculpture this influence was no more than an initial stimulus which helped to create something entirely new. Music, however, seems to have been literally 'imported' into Greece from abroad. This is evident from the Greek myths connected with the origins of music; from some names employed in musical terminology; and from the musical instruments in use. Two of the principal modes are termed Lydian and Phrygian after two countries in Asia Minor. The lyre was introduced from Thrace; the cythara and aulos from Asia Minor; and many other instruments were called 'foreign' by the Greeks themselves. But the way music became an integral part of everyday life, of religion, education, and even politics, is something eminently Greek.

Music was the main element in the Greek educational system. In Athens, Sparta and Thebes everybody had to learn to play the aulos. Every child was instructed in the use of the principal instruments. And at social gatherings the lyre was often handed round and every guest was expected, and was able, to contribute to the singing to the accompaniment of the lyre.

Compared with the thousands of monuments of architecture, sculpture and the applied arts, and with the many volumes of literature and poetry that have survived from ancient Greece, the handful of musical monuments that have come down to us are sad relics of an art which was of such prime importance in Greek civilisation. They include several hymns, an ode by Pindar, a fragment of a choral song from one of Euripides' plays, and a funerary song inscribed on a grave stele in Thracles in Asia Minor.

It is from works of art like the Brygos vessel that we can at least learn much

2. DIONYSUS AND THE DANCING SATYRS
Bibliothèque Nationale, Paris

Attic Cup. By the 'Painter of Brygos'.
Beginning of 5th century BC.

about the musical instruments employed in ancient Greece; and in works of such expressive power as this masterpiece, something perhaps of the nature and spirit of their music.

E.R.

Fig. 2. *Detail showing the Aulos, from an Attic Cup representing the Banquet of Simkros.*

chorus of the Dionysian festivals. Even the art of acting had its origins in the transformation effected during this religious ecstasy. It is not strange, therefore, that it was Dionysus who presided over the great festivals of Greek drama.

The Greeks must have been extraordinarily sensitive to music, otherwise they would not have attached so much importance to the moral effect that this or that mode might have upon Athenian youth. Socrates in his scheme for education rejected certain modes on the grounds that they were 'expressive of sorrow', and others because they were likely to encourage 'drunkenness, softness and indolence'. On the other hand, other modes, such as the Dorian and Phrygian, were approved.

In the same way that the various modes were thought to possess individual ethical character, specific powers were attributed to the different instruments. Thus the aulos (Fig. 2) was mainly an instrument for music that roused the senses; the lyre and cythara, the instruments for lyric and epic music. The epics of Homer, for instance, were sung to the accompaniment of the cythara. The vase by the 'Painter of Brygos' shows, however, that the dividing lines were not too strict. In this painting which depicts Dionysus in a state of ecstasy, we can surely imagine how the participants of his cult shared in this 'sacred madness'. There can be few works of art which express so forcefully the transforming power of music.

Elizabeth Rosenbaum

Bibliography

Erwin Rohde
Psyche
Freiburg i.B, 1894

G. M. A. Richter
A Handbook of Greek Art
Phaidon Press, London, 1959

R. M. Cook
Greek painted pottery
Methuen, London, 1960

3 Dancing Girl and Musicians

Wall painting, Ajanta Caves, India 6th century AD

THIS PAINTING from the Buddhist cave temples of Ajanta, believed to date from the sixth century AD, is part of a large fresco covering one of the walls of Cave I, the most splendid of the cave temples at Ajanta. It is painted with the simplest of materials – lamp-black, red and yellow ochre and lapis lazuli are the predominent pigments used.

The whole wall-painting evokes – rather than narrates – a well-known tale, choosing three moments, or three moods, in the story. The first, of which Plate 3 reproduces a part, takes place in the precincts of a palace built around three wooden pavilions, the lines of which help to create the sense of space. In the pearl-hung pavilion at the top left sit the meditative king and his graceful queen, surrounded by their retinue. The eye moves diagonally forwards and downwards through a middle pavilion, where stands a girl watching a dancer in the third pavilion at the bottom.

On the left (immediately to the left of the scene reproduced in the Plate) sits a woman in the royal pavilion, her face turned to watch the dancer. On the right, a girl leans against a pillar, absorbed. Framed by these two figures the dancer rises out of her band of musicians. To her right are two girls playing the flute. To her left are two girls standing with cymbals in their hands, and two seated playing drums, one with a pair of upright drums like the modern Indian *dhōl*, and the other, sitting cross-legged, with a drum held horizontally, like the modern *mirdang*. A fifth, with her back to us, has on her lap what might be a gourd, perhaps part of a string instrument.

The softly rounded limbs of the figures seem to flow outwards towards us, yet they are far away, immersed in their own vision, caught up in a profound concentration as they produce their music with the flute, the drum and the cymbal. The bells on the wrists and ankles of the dancer emphasize her movements as she stamps her feet and moves her wrists to the short repetitive beats of the rhythm.

Each figure is united to the other through the music they are producing. They are brought together not only because they are within the lacquered and carved pillars of the pavilion, but because they are, as it were, embraced together, arrested in their movements by their collective act in creating music. Each individual is alone with his own performance and yet completely united to the others.

Music is there, in the attitude of each head, in the lines of the robes, the curves of the bodies, the sloping forms of the drums standing to the right of the dancer, in the jewels swinging carelessly, the floating ribbons, the pensive listener leaning against the pillar to the right, the swirling figure of the dancer in the centre. If one listens, one can hear the music and be caught up in it, penetrating into the enchanted world created on the face of this rock.

The posture of the dancer and the instruments that accompany her are very similar to what we see in India today. The technique of Indian music and dance is one of evocation and suggestion within a complex structure of shared attitudes. The words of the lyric allude to some familiar situation. The melody is improvised within accepted musical modes, and set to rhythms that are again variations improvised by the drummers within a defined pattern. The dancer dances to the rhythm, and in her turn improvises within an accepted language of gesture. Together they create a mood, composing the music and dance in concert. In the present painting, the composition of the small, closed

Fig. 3a. *Drummer.*

Fig. 3b. *Flute Player.*

Fig. 3c. *Dancer.*

Figs. 3a–c. *Details from a medieval stone relief, Southern India.*

3. DANCING GIRL AND MUSICIANS
Victoria and Albert Museum, London

Copy after a detail from a wall painting.
Ajanta Caves, India. 6th century AD.

The cave temples at Ajanta and their decoration, dating in greater part to the Gupta Period (*c.* 320 – *c.* 647), the 'Golden Age' of Indian art, count among the greatest works produced in the whole history of Indian painting. As a large decorative scheme its importance in Indian art is perhaps comparable to that of Michelangelo's decoration of the Sistine Chapel in European art. The most famous paintings and the most splendid, are those decorating Cave I, the largest and architecturally the finest of the temples. All the interiors of these temples – the columns, walls and ceilings – are covered with paintings, much of the painting now unfortunately lost. In recent years some of the painted surfaces have disappeared. Plate 3 reproduces a careful copy made of the frescoes before more recent depredations. Unfortunately, although more complete and more easily legible, the copy necessarily loses much of the quality of the original.

Bibliography

Stella Kramrisch
The Art of India
Phaidon Press, London, 1954

G. Yazdani
Ajanta
Oxford University Press, Oxford, 1930

E. B. Cowell and W. H. D. Ronse (trans.)
The Jataka or Stories of the Buddha's former births
Cambridge University Press,
Cambridge, 1907

group conveys an intimate and self-sufficient unity. The eyes of the dancer herself are turned inwards in rapt ecstasy.

The whole wall-painting illustrates the *Mahajanaka Jataka* (a story from the *Jataka*, the tales of the previous incarnations of the Buddha) which tells of a man marked out to attain wisdom. The composition wanders up and down the wall returning again to the centre, to the scene of the pavilions and the dancer, like a melody returning upon itself.

The tale tells of the king Janaka, blessed by good fortune, happily married to his queen Sivali, and with his seven hundred favourite concubines. While riding out on his elephant in the royal garden, he received the insight which led him to choose 'the barren life' and 'wander through the woods, eating of their hospitable fruit, tuning my heart in solitude as one might tune a seven-stringed lute'. 'I had no teacher', says king Janaka; but in the garden he saw two trees, one laden with mango fruit and the other covered only with foliage 'as beautiful as a mountain of gems'. From the first tree he tasted a mango, from which a divine flavour seemed to arise, and he promised himself more on his way back. But after the king had eaten this fruit, his retinue attacked the tree for its fruit, and when he returned the tree stood despoiled. The king was greatly moved:

'The fruitful tree stood there, forlorn,
Its leaves all stripped, its branches bare.
The barren tree stood green and strong,
Its foliage waving in the air.
We kings are like that fruitful tree . . .
That pair of trees my teachers were'.

He decides to become an ascetic. Queen Sivali arranges for concubines to dance before him (this is the scene of our Plate), but to no purpose. He rides out on his horse to the northern mountains.

Here is expressed this single-minded devotion to renunciation combined with an exquisite awareness of the beauty of the world – sensuous beauty is represented in all its fulness and self-sufficiency. In contrast to Hindu aesthetics, which sees in music and dance a mode of approach to the divine, the Buddhist attitude is to see in these things the temptations of the senses that prevent the practice of the strictest discipline, through which alone the human being achieves a true vision of the world and of nature. The whole composition conveys the movement and the stillness of music and dance, as well as the movement and stillness of life that moves inexorably to its goal of Nirvana. This is the total melody of the painting, in which the actual musicians play an integral part.

Sita Narasimhan

4 Celestial Musicians

Stone relief from the Stupa of Borobudor, Java, Indonesia. 750–800

THIS GROUP is a detail from the long frieze decorating the upper gallery of the great Buddhist stupa at Borobudor. The frieze is part of a great series of reliefs depicting the life of the Buddha which the faithful would look at as they slowly ascended each succeeding terrace to the top in the 'Pradakshina', the ritual walk round a sacred site.

The composition from which this group of musicians is taken (Fig. 4) shows the Buddha in the Tushita heaven before he descends to earth in human form. Though the musicians are heavenly beings, the artist has portrayed them as extremely human, drawing from his experience and observation of life. This approach is typical of the style of the period, and the art of Borobudor is acknowledged as one of the most striking examples of naturalism in the whole history of art.

Our first impression when we look at the group is one of uniformity. There is no accented articulation of the individual figures or the group, no abrupt transitions of the forms, but a calm flow, an even smoothness of surface of the relief. The individual figures and the group appear eternally young or ageless. It is very different from any sculptural group in Western art, in which the eye strikes upon strong accents, or where muscular tension may be emphasized. What is it then that makes this relief so alive? It is not the individual characterisation of each figure that brings it to life. As in nearly all Asian art, one has to look again and again before the work of art reveals its true character.

The stupa of Borobudor, built between 750 and 800 AD, consists of six superimposed terraces, the lowest terrace some 480 feet square. At the four cardinal points of the compass there are placed flights of steps with gateways. The whole structure is covered with small stupas, and is crowned with a central stupa 52 feet in diameter.

The lower part of the building is regarded as symbolic of the world and the life of the senses; the uppermost part (which is unadorned), as symbolic of the world of the mind.

Apart from the rows of reliefs, there are hundreds of images of the Buddha and other statues.

The art of Borobudor is entirely original, and at the same time it is the finest example of Indo-Javanese art. The Sailendra kings, probably of Indian origin from Sumatra, conquered central Java around 675 to 750, and the monuments dating from their reign (750–900) belong to what is called Central Java-

Fig. 4. *The Buddha in the Tushita heaven. The group of Celestial Musicians appears at bottom left.*

4. CELESTAIL MUSICIANS
Stupa of Borobudor, Java.

Detail from the stone reliefs of the Stupa of Borobudor, Java, Indonesia.
750-800.

nese art. There was at this time continuous contact with India, and affinities exist between the medieval art of Bengal (India) and Central Javanese art. The Buddhist kings of Java had even built hostels to house their pilgrims and students who went to study at the Buddhist University of Nalanda in Bengal; while the Chinese scholar I-Ching studied Sanskrit at the University of Palembang in Sumatra in the seventh century, and informs us that the stories from the life of the Buddha were extremely popular in the Indonesian islands. The Indians visited the islands as traders and missionaries, and soon settled there and intermarried with the inhabitants of the islands.

A. de S.

The group is diverse, yet in complete harmony; each face and figure is like a note of music making up a melody. They come to life for us with a gentle grace that seems to flow like the music they are making; and the intense absorption in their performance binds them together excluding all else around them. These celestial musicians form a compact group apart from the rest of the relief – belonging together as a group only through their music. The play of light and shadow on the movement of their heads and limbs, the rhythm made by the fall of their jewels, the curve of their girdles and the upward sweep of their head-dresses, are all part of this harmony.

The vitality derives from the variation in expression, however subtly or gently it is done. The flautist to the right is playing a solo, accompanied by the string instrument to the left; the player in the middle who holds the lute has, perhaps, just finished the last of his accompanying phrases and turns towards the player next to him, listening and waiting for the moment when he should join the music again; the player behind leans forward intently so that he may not lose the slightest signal to go on. The profound feeling and the seriousness with which the Javanese approached their music and the particular excellence of their orchestral music – which still persists – could only be produced by the sense of dedication and concentration that this relief implies. The penetrating charm and tenderness which pervades the Buddhist art of Borobudor, and this relief in particular, is typical of the delicate, supple and tranquil grace of the art of Central Java from the eighth to the tenth century. The absence of tension in the modelling in high relief is offset by a very human warmth and tenderness. The late A. K. Coomaraswamy wrote that 'there is no nervous tension, no concentration of force to be compared with that which so impresses the observer at Angkor Vat*. Borobudor is like a ripe fruit, matured in a breathless air. The fulness of its forms is an expression of static wealth rather than a volume that denotes the outward radiation of power'. Another description: 'at Angkor it is all activity, whereas at Borobudor it is all repose'.

The link that was forged between the daily life of the Javanese people and their art is still evident. In various parts of Indonesia, particularly in the lovely island of Bali, 'music permeates their life to a degree which we can hardly imagine, a music of incomparable subtlety and intricacy, yet as simple as breathing' (de Zoete). 'Day and night the air is vibrant with the golden metallic sounds of the Gamelan (orchestra peculiar to Java and Bali) accompanying either religious ceremony or the performance of dance and drama. Children sit on their fathers' knees in the Gamelan before they can walk, and their tiny hands strike the cymbals or metal keys, or hold the drum sticks . . . it almost seems that they absorb directly into their bodies the melodies and the complicated rhythms, just as they absorb the rhythms and postures of the dance' (Mehee).

Perhaps in no other part of the world is music, dance and drama more intimately linked: the dancer 'conveys the moods of the music, and the music lives and has its fullest expression in and through the dancer', while drama is born when dialogues are carried on between the dancers during certain rituals.

When we again look at this relief, echoes come to us over the centuries of a civilisation which gave its people a pattern of daily life filled with golden sound, making of each peasant a potential artist, giving each man, woman and child the daily possibility of poetic expression.

Anil de Silva

Bibliography

A. K. Coomaraswamy
History of Indian and Indonesian Art
London, 1927

Reginald Le May
The Culture of South-East Asia
Allen and Unwin, London, 1954

Heinrich Zimmer
The Art of Indian Asia
Pantheon Books, Bollingen Series, New York, 1955

*Angkor Vat is discussed in *Man Through His Art*, Vol. 1, *War and Peace*, Plate 8.

5 Procession of Musicians

Fresco from Bonampak Temple, Mexico. 8th–9th century

THE PAINTING represents a group of musicians, dressed in festival array, participating in a ceremony of thanksgiving to the gods for a victory in war over their enemy. This particular group belongs to the percussion section of the musical procession. Three men shake their large rattles; the others beat upon their drums made of turtle-shells. In the upper part of the fresco is a band of Mayan hieroglyphics, a language which experts are only barely beginning to decipher today.

More than four centuries ago, when the Spanish conquerors disembarked on the shores of what is now Mexico, they found themselves confronted with a civilisation of extraordinary and totally unexpected beauty. Shining white cities, built around towering pyramids, bore evidence of a long and flourishing artistic tradition, in which Music and its companion the Dance played an outstanding role.

Little is known today about the music of ancient Mexico, but thanks to many carefully preserved wall-paintings and sculptures we do know something of the instruments used at the many festivals; and also from the prominence these unknown painters and sculptors of long ago gave to music, we may appreciate the importance attached to the art by this distant civilisation.

In ancient Mexico, music was not considered a separate art, but was developed as an essential part of the profound religious ritual that governed the lives of the people, giving meaning to each act, thought and gesture from birth to their ceremonious death. No celebration or ritual could be conceived without music, without the beat of drums to accentuate and stir the pulse, combined with the lyric melodies of wind instruments to express that wide range of feeling that found its highest fulfilment in the human voice.

The instruments we find portrayed in the paintings and sculptures of ancient Mexico belong to the percussion and wind groups, and were made from a variety of materials, including shells, sugar-cane and clay. Among the wind instruments were long reed pipes and smaller clay whistles that imitated the chirping of birds, the murmur of the sea and other sounds of nature. Whistles were also made from human bones, more especially the humerus, and *ocarinas* from shells pierced with small holes. Many different kinds of drums were used: some, very large, were made of animal hide and wood; others were made from the shells of turtles, over which snake-skins were stretched, as in the present painting. The drums produced powerful reverberations that could be heard over long distances. The musicians also used a variety of rattles, of which one type appears on this painting, and scrapers to accent the rhythm.

Some of these ancient instruments from the Mayan and Aztec cultures are preserved in the National Museum of Mexico, and experts have concluded that the music played upon them must have been of an extremely simple kind, limited in range to possibly a scale of five notes. Similar music, played on almost identical instruments, can still be heard in remote Indian villages in Mexico where tradition has kept alive, generation after generation, songs and dances that must have had their origin in ancient times; and anyone who has travelled into the innermost regions of Mexico and heard this strange music played upon primitive drums and pipes knows how poignant and expressive it can be, for it seems to touch that inexhaustible well of creative inspiration, man's communion with Nature. Nowadays, as centuries ago, wherever tradition remains pure, Mexican music seems to commune with Nature, to speak to the birds in the air, to answer the cry of a frightened child. It is a music that sings with the voice of forgotten ancestors.

Fortunately, there came to the New World with the Spanish conquerors

The original wall-paintings are to be found in Bonampak, in the State of Chiapas, Mexico – Bonampak in Mayan means the 'temple of the wall-paintings'. Archaeologists believe that the temple was decorated some time between the eighth and ninth century AD. For centuries the paintings were hidden beneath dense jungle, their existence known only to a few inhabitants of the region. In 1945, a group of archaeologists finally penetrated inside the three chambers of this temple built upon a pyramid, and uncovered examples of an art that has thrown new light upon the entire Mayan civilisation.

Plate 5 reproduces a copy of the original Bonampak Temple paintings made by the archaeologist and painter Agustín Villagra. Due to the climate of Chiapas, of intense heat and long rainy seasons, the original paintings have already lost much of their colour, and in some parts the figures have begun to disappear. It was therefore necessary to make a copy so that a record of this remarkable treasure would be preserved for future generations to enjoy.

G.F.

5. PROCESSION OF MUSICIANS
Bonampak Temple, Mexico

Detail from a wall painting.
Bonampak Temple, Mexico. 8th-9th century.

several missionaries who wrote down their colourful and detailed descriptions of this civilisation, with its cities of pyramids and observatories built to study the skies. Diego Durán, in his *Historia de las Indias*, tells us that in every city, next to the temples, there stood large houses called '*cuicacalli*', or 'Houses of Song', where professors of music, song and dance trained young people in these arts so that they might have the professional finish required of the ballet and choral groups that participated in the constant rituals and celebrations. There were songs and dances of great solemnity, with a rhythm measured and austere; others, for less serious occasions, were lighter and sang of love and happiness. Most elaborate of all were those that accompanied the floral offerings to the gods. The richness of the costumes imitating fruits and flowers, birds and animals; the grace of the dancers representing the gods and their worshippers; and the strange and stirring music, all made Durán declare that this was 'the most beautiful and solemn dance this nation possessed', and he never expected to witness again anything more wondrous.

A feeling of elaborate ritual and of great solemnity, accentuated by the colourful costumes and strange instruments, springs forcefully from this painting, depicting the celebration of a recent victory in war.

Gisèle Freund

Bibliography

Dr. Gisele Freund
Mexique Précolumbien
Ides et Calendes, Neuchâtel and Paris, 1954

S. K. Lothrop, W. F. Foshag and Joy Mahler
Pre-Columbian Art
Phaidon Press, London, 1957

6 The South Transept of Lausanne Cathedral

Switzerland. *c.* **1220**

IN THIS SERIES of masterpieces, we encounter some surprising representations of music in the visual arts. Thus an Indian miniature is found to depict a mood conceived to be identical with a musical mode (Plate 15). In order to understand this work, we had to appreciate the possible correspondence between a musical composition and the inner disposition of the listener, a correspondence reflected in the connection between the words 'mode' and 'mood' in most western languages.

A very different experience of music, though one quite as surprising to most of us, is evoked by the architectural masterpiece in Plate 6. We are looking at the inner wall of the south transept of Lausanne Cathedral. It must have been executed before 1235, because we find a drawing of the rose window in the book of architectural models compiled about that time by the French architect Villard de Honnecourt. Architecture has sometimes been referred to as 'frozen music', but if we could ask the master builder of Lausanne in what sense his work was musical, he would have given us a very specific answer, calling our attention to the correspondence between the proportions of his facade and those musical consonances that he and his contemporaries considered more perfect than any other.

Fig. 6a. *Schematic diagram of the Rose Window at Lausanne Cathedral.*

Of what does this correspondence, this affinity between visual proportion and audible consonance, consist? If you take a chord and divide it into two, the half chord will sound a tone exactly one octave above that produced by the whole. This octave relationship then can be expressed by the ratio 1:2. Similarly, the consonance of the fifth and the fourth correspond to the ratios 2:3 and 3:4. To the musical aesthetics of the Middle Ages, which were based on the celebrated treatise on Music by St. Augustine, the founder of medieval aesthetics, these consonances were more perfect than any others, because they depended on simple ratios, approaching the principle of oneness. Even more perfect than these consonances, according to St. Augustine, was that of unison, with its ratio of one to one. Medieval music attests to this preference for the 'perfect' consonances; but we must bear in mind that the reason is not its particularly agreeable sound. Rather did the sound recall to medieval man a metaphysical truth – the unity which was the source and centre of all creation.

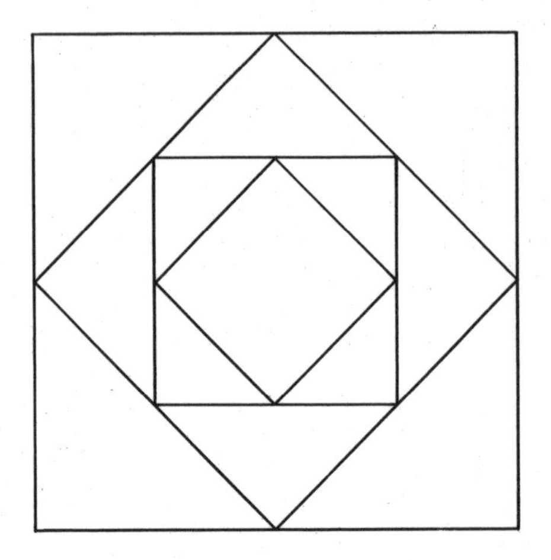

Figs. 6b and c. *Diagrams from the notebook of Villard de Honnecourt, illustrating a sequence of expanding squares.*

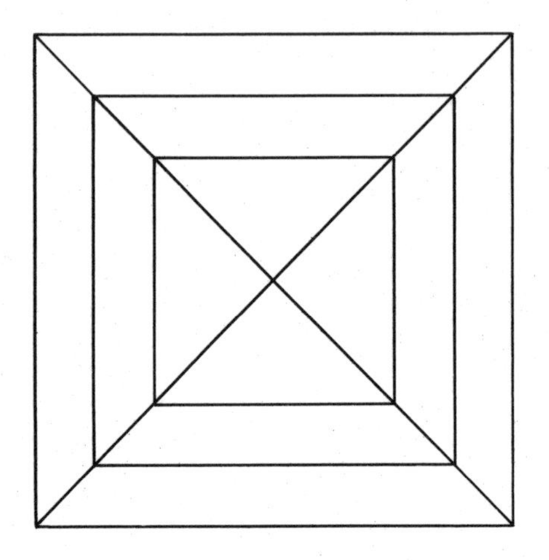

Musical beauty to medieval man was thus an echo of metaphysical truth; and visual beauty had to be the mirror of that truth. The ratios that to St. Augustine accounted for the perfection of the consonances mentioned would be expressed visually by the division of a line or a surface corresponding to those of the chord we have mentioned.

The resulting proportions, 1:1; 1:2; 2:3, were felt to be as pleasing to the eye as the corresponding consonances were to the ear and for the same reason. That is why St. Augustine and his pupils considered architecture, the art of geometrical proportion, the sister of music. And it is for this reason that the proportions mentioned occur so frequently in medieval architecture. If we look at the Lausanne transept wall we find that the horizontal cornice below the rose window divides the entire height, from the floor to the apex of the great enveloping arch, exactly in the ratio 1:1. Moreover, the distance between this cornice and the one below it is twice the distance between this lower cornice and the floor. Thus the three horizontal parts of the wall relate to one another as 1:2:3, 'sounding' the perfect consonances: unison, octave, fifth. Does not the wonderful simplicity of this architectural composition convey to our eyes the experience of harmony in music?

But we must go a step further and consider the great rose window itself. Geometrically, as our diagram shows (Fig. 6a), its design is based on squares;

6. THE SOUTH TRANSEPT OF LAUSANNE CATHEDRAL *Ca.* 1220.
Lausanne, Switzerland

the area of each succeeding square being twice that of the preceding one. This device occurs with extraordinary frequency in Gothic architecture, and we have reason to believe that the architects of that age considered it the most important ruling geometrical principle of their art. The architect Villard de Honnecourt, already mentioned, shows us such a sequence in his note-book (Figs. 6b and 6c).

The reason is not hard to find. With its sides related as 1:1, the square introduces, as it were, the principle of unison into the world of geometrical forms. The sequence of expanding squares referred to could be carried out with the help of cord and pegs even by the unlearned stone-mason, the diagonal of each square producing a square twice its area. This sequence then will yield squares related as 1:2:4:8, a chain of 'octave' ratios. This chain to the medieval mind had a significance that cannot be ignored in the present context. The Middle Ages conceived the cosmos as a kind of musical universe, a symphony composed of an infinite variety of individual parts related to one another by the harmony of musical proportion. The source of this thought was Plato, whose philosophy dominated more than a thousand years of Christian thinking. Plato's famous cosmological treatise, *Timaeus*, was well known throughout the Middle Ages. Now in *Timaeus*, Plato taught that the primary bodies of which the world is composed are to be thought of as building materials which the divine architect puts together in accordance with the perfect geometrical proportions of squares and cubes.

According to Platonic tradition, the simple ratios of the musical consonances are not only elements of aesthetic beauty, but also scientific laws that assure the stability and order of the Universe. And by these laws the medieval architect had to abide, just as the modern architect has to abide by the laws of science. Hence, the extremely important role that geometry plays in medieval architecture, not only in design, like the rose window in Lausanne, but as a structural principle, governing the ground plan as well as the elevation of a building. But nowhere was the rule of geometry, the geometry of 'musical' proportions, more called for than in the medieval sanctuary, since like the sacred buildings of other great civilisations such as India, the medieval church was conceived as an image of the cosmos.

In the central square of the rose window (Plate 6 and Fig. 6a) appears the representation of the year surrounded by the sun and moon, day and night. In each of the four lobes adjoining each side of the square are represented the four seasons, each with its three corresponding months; and within the outer circles, between these lobes, are the four elements and the signs of the Zodiac. In the corners of the larger square appear the Four Rivers of Paradise, each flanked by a pair of strange human beings representing legendary people thought to live at the extreme confines of the world. Eight winds are finally depicted along the periphery of the great circle. Here, then, we behold the entire cosmos; but as we noted above, in the perfect order of a geometrical pattern composed of the 'octave' sequence of squares. Never has man represented the symphony of all creation in a more adequate composition.

Otto von Simson

Bibliography

Otto von Simson
The Gothic Cathedral
Kegan Paul, London, 1956 and 1962 and Pantheon Books, Bollingen Series, New York, 1956

Ellen J. Beer
Die Rose der Katedrale von Lausanne
Benteli, Berne, 1952

7 Christ glorified in the Court of Heaven

Panel painting by Fra Angelico, Italy. *c.* 1430

PLATE 7 reproduces the central panel (little more than 12 inches in height) of a range of five panels making up one long composition, *Christ glorified in the Court of Heaven* (Fig. 7a), which originally graced the *predella*, or base, of the high altarpiece of the church of the Dominican friary of San Domenico near Fiesole in Tuscany, where the devout artist had early taken his vows and stayed, eventually as prior, until his death. The central panel represents the Christ of the Resurrection surrounded by the angelic host, a gentle and fervent throng through whose serried ranks move waves of adoration. The angels appear all as musicians, contributing their voices and the chords of a whole array of exquisite musical instruments to this one great surge of adoration. The uppermost range of angels contribute only the silent music of their earnest devotion. Indeed it is difficult to describe the music of this heavenly orchestra and choir in terms of sound; it is an infinitely pure and happy music directed to the heavens, to our Creator, and certainly the sound is not of music of this earth. It is a music to which we can contribute, even silently, our own voices, but which is not directed to us, is not for our entertainment. Perhaps it is of every sincere work of art to involve us rather than entertain us.

The music of this painting depends in only a very limited way upon the inclusion of the musical instruments, though their variety and their exquisite design are, necessarily, completely in sympathy with all else that makes up the painting, that contributes to the final expression; and likewise their disposition in this carefully worked-out composition. The whole composition formed by the five panels of the *predella* builds up to its culmination in this central panel in which painting seems to dematerialise and be transformed into music. It is only in this panel that instruments play and voices sing, but the other panels are essential to the building up to this great climax.

The immediate impression of this apparently simple, balanced composition is one of serenity. The balance and composure of the design make it almost inevitable that we follow the measured rhythm, pause at the measured intervals, until the composition reaches its climax, much in the way that we follow music; but in the painting, the separate notes, the separate chords, are here the things of the visual artist. The composition uses the elements of a carefully graded colour scheme, a variation in mass and shape and pose, a variation and accumulation of motifs in space, and a gentle but gradually increasing rhythmic movement which leads from the outer panels towards the central panel.

The figures in the outer, squarish panels to the extreme left and right of the *predella* are dressed in the black and white of the Dominican Order – they are the beatified of Fra Angelico's own Order – kneeling and turned towards the centre, they little more than indicate the direction the movement is to take. Their almost static figures are comparatively loosely spaced in three rows.

Following the pause created by the transition to the adjoining, longer panels, the movement is taken up and gains gradually in quiet urgency. In these panels delicate primary colours are gradually introduced – blue, rose, yellow, green – interspersed at first with the black and white, and also brown, of the robes until the middle of the panel is reached, where again there is a short interval. Following this interval all are pure primary colours. In these longer panels, which include the ancestors of Christ on the right and the Apostles and the Virgin on the left, the increasingly lighter and more lively rhythm is exactly consonant with the mutation in the colour, and the figures too are somewhat smaller and lighter, and the three tiers close up as the figures press gently towards the central panel. Each head is surrounded by a

Fig. 7a. *Fra Angelico. The predella representing* Christ glorified in the Court of Heaven *(central panel, reproduced on Plate 7, omitted here).*

7. CHRIST GLORIFIED IN THE COURT OF HEAVEN
National Gallery, London

Fra Angelico. *Ca.* 1430.
Panel painting. $12\frac{1}{2}$ x $28\frac{3}{4}$ in.: 32 x 73 cm.

Fra Angelico, Florentine painter, born about 1380, died 1455. He entered the San Domenico friary near Fiesole in 1407 and stayed there, eventually as prior, until his death. The name Angelico appears to have been given him after his death, and also, although he does not appear to have been beatified, the epithet 'Beato', in acknowledgement of his unquestionable piety which is borne out in all his paintings.

Nothing is known of his training but he certainly learnt much from both Lorenzo Monaco and Masaccio.

Lorenzo Monaco born before 1372 in Siena, died in 1422 or later. Like Fra Angelico, Lorenzo Monaco was a member of a religious Order, belonging to the Camaldolese monastery in Florence. He was first recorded as a painter in 1399. His attractive decorative style of painting is representative of the so-called International Gothic style of the late fourteenth and early fifteenth century.

Masaccio, Florentine painter, born 1401, died 1427–9. He was the great pioneer of Renaissance painting. His revolutionary style, grave and monumental, is exemplified in the grand series of frescoes in the Brancacci Chapel in the Carmelite Church of Florence, and in the high altarpiece of the Carmelite Church in Pisa, of which the *Madonna and Child Enthroned* reproduced in the text (Fig. 7c) formed the main panel.

Fig. 7b. *Lorenzo Monaco. Detail of* The Coronation of the Virgin. *c.*1415.

golden halo, in place of the golden rays of the beatified in the preceding panels, increasing the colourful quality.

Immediately before one passes to the central panel there is again a hiatus, now respectfully longer. In the central panel, the figures of the angels, in six tiers (or, perhaps, four – the lowest range three deep) instead of three, are smaller, lighter and throng more closely together, and the robes of these almost floating figures are painted in more delicate shades of rose, blue and

Fig. 7c. *Masaccio.* The Virgin and Child Enthroned. *c.*1426.

green, the uppermost range in shades of rose alone (on the left) and blue (on the right). Each angel wears his golden halo and wings ornamented in gold. In sympathy with all this their draperies take up a delightful rhythm that moves towards the centre, gently halting against the expanse of gold incised with the rays emanating from the central figure of Christ clothed in white – the only white on this panel. Only the lowest range of angels carry a little further this gliding rhythm which is continued in the long, slender trumpets finally to enter as music the central glory surrounding the Creator, and to become resolved too in the circular movement of the two angels with small manual organs kneeling below the great central aureole.

It is indeed difficult to cite any other painting that so serenely expresses the act of adoration as a selfless offering. As the painter makes this offering one senses no display or even awareness of his skill as an artist and craftsman. That he makes his offering as music seems to be inevitable and in no way contrived. The newly reformed Order of the Dominican Observance to which the artist belonged insisted on a simplicity of devotion, and acknowledged the practice of painting as a devotional exercise.

Whilst the subject of the painting has not been precisely identified, everything that is recognisable is consonant with a reference to the Preface of Easter and the Sanctus (the hymn concluding the Easter service): 'It is truly meet . . . that at all times, but more especially on this day . . . we should extol thy Glory, O Lord . . . who by dying hath overcome our death and by rising again hath restored our life. And therefore, with Angels and Archangels, with Thrones and Dominions, and with all the heavenly hosts, we sing a hymn to thy Glory, saying without ceasing: Holy, holy, holy – Lord God of Hosts. Heaven and earth are full of thy Glory . . .'. The Risen Christ glorified by the hosts is appropriate; the Archangel Michael at least can be recognised; and the four tiers of angels must certainly refer to the four hierarchies of Angels of the Preface. But, above all, there could hardly be a closer correspondence between the spirit expressed in the Preface and Sanctus and that expressed in the painting.

Fra Angelico lived at the end of the Middle Ages and the dawn of the New Age, and his spirit and his art owes something to both. There is something of the medieval spirit in the unquestioning character of his devotion, and as a painter he certainly learned much from such a master as Lorenzo Monaco, his elder contemporary, and one of the great exponents of the International Gothic style. There is, however, in his painting nothing of the superficial, decorative quality of this charming, aristocratic style which closed the Middle Ages; nothing of the so precious, thin music which we see expressed in Monaco's comparable masterpiece of similar date (Fig. 7b). From the great pioneer of the Early Renaissance, Masaccio, his younger contemporary, he certainly learned more (Fig. 7c; this early masterpiece of Renaissance painting predates Fra Angelico's painting by some five years), but there was in Fra Angelico's painting nothing of the latent spirit of questioning or of self-confidence of the New Age.

Philip Troutman

Bibliography

John Pope-Hennessy
Fra Angelico
Phaidon Press, London, 1951

8 Stream, Mountains and Secluded Fishermen

Detail from an illuminated scroll by T'ang Yin, China. Early 16th century

ON A WARM DAY at the beginning of autumn, two gentlemen sit in their boats on the river. One, his wine-jar close to hand, is playing the flute (*hsiao*), cooling his toes in the current; he looks contentedly across to his friend in the other boat, who leans back on a bundle of scrolls, clapping his hands in time to the music. A gentle breeze has shaken down the first red leaves of autumn, and they lie on the ground and on the water. The high, thin notes of the flute are blended with the sound of the wind and waterfall in a natural harmony that is uniquely Chinese.

Elsewhere in the long handscroll of which this is only a small part, we see other scholars fishing (or rather, making fishing an excuse for spending an idle day on the river), or gazing out from a terrace over the water, or strolling in a garden by the riverside. At the end of it, T'ang Yin has written this four-line verse:

'With tea-stove and fishing-rod we nourish our free souls;
Far stretches the stream, and dark is the trees' shade.
Now is a time of peace, when heroes are idle.
The water is unconfined, and the grassy pools are deep.'

In this most poetic of landscapes, the branches of the trees and the outlines of the rocks play against each other in a lively rhythm. The separate brush-strokes are angular and precise, yet infinitely sensitive. In modelling his rocks, T'ang Yin has used two quite different techniques: in the left foreground, the 'axe-cut' texture strokes derived from the twelfth-century painter Li T'ang; in the background, he leaves light areas resembling brush-strokes between patches of dark ink, a technique developed by his master Chou Ch'en. This complex ink technique is combined with warm autumn colours to create a wonderfully rich yet tranquil harmony.

T'ang Yin spent his life in and around the city of Soochow in Kiangsu. He was trained for an official career, but became involved with a friend who cheated in the government examinations, and was disgraced. Thereafter he found consolation in painting, in wine and women, and in periodic retreats to a Zen monastery. Too poor to retire, he supported himself with his brush. There was a great demand for his pictures, many of which, like this one, depict the life of cultivated ease which was denied to him.

T'ang Yin's scholarly friends, painting only to please themselves and each other, expressed themselves in an abstract, calligraphic style in terms of ink alone. T'ang Yin was obliged to please a wider public. His style consequently has elements of professionalism in it. There is a conscious elegance, even a hint of mannerism, in his brush-work; his colouring too is more naturalistic and alluring than that in the landscapes of his scholar friends such as Wen Cheng-ming, who often dispensed with colour altogether. Yet his pictures are in perfect taste, and his mastery of drawing, design and colour is complete. T'ang Yin thus occupies a place in Ming Dynasty painting mid-way between the rather abstract ink painting of the scholars and the colourful, realistic style of the acknowledged professionals and academicians.

The theme of scholars at their ease in peaceful rural surroundings is one of the most popular in Chinese painting. But such pictures were not merely conventional or traditional; they satisfied a deeply-felt need. In China, a man with a classical education was a member of the elite. His Confucian sense of duty obliged him to devote his life to public service. Often, burdened with routine administration or cares of state, he would long to get away from it all, to wander in the woods with his friends, or fish idly in some mountain stream. When his work made escape impossible, he could still find time to gather a few friends together over a cup of wine, unroll a landscape handscroll such as this,

T'ang Yin was born 1470 and died 1523.

There were two kinds of scrolls, the vertical and the horizontal. The first was intended to hang unrolled. The horizontal scroll, or hand-scroll, was designed to be held and unrolled in the hand, and to be 'read' from right to left. Thus the element of time was introduced into the paintings, which were deliberately composed for one part to be seen at a time. The art of scroll.painting originated in China. In our painting, which is a detail of a hand-scroll, a bundle of scrolls can be seen in one of the boats.

8. STREAM, MOUNTAINS AND SECLUDED FISHERMEN
The National Palace Museums, Taiwan

T'ang Yin. Early 16th century.
From a Chinese scroll painting. $11\frac{1}{2}$ x $13\frac{3}{4}$ in.: 29 x 35 cm.

and take an imaginary stroll through the countryside. It was not necessary that such paintings should depict real places; but in order that they should give him refreshment of mind and spirit, it was essential that they should have the power to arouse in him the same *kind* of feelings that he would have were he to wander in a real landscape.

T'ang Yin achieves this by creating a typical autumn scene, beyond the accidents of time and place. Years of practice with the brush, like the pianist's exercises, have given him not only manual skill, but also a repertory of typical forms for rocks and trees, on which he can draw at will. Though these are traditional, he has added to them something of his own, and has vitalised them by the creative energy of his brush-work. Thus his painting not only evokes the essential character of rocks and trees, but breathes life into them as well. The men for whom this picture was painted could easily imagine themselves listening to the waterfall and the plaintive notes of the flute. Such is the charm of T'ang Yin's art that, wherever we may be, we too can join them on the river-bank.

Michael Sullivan

Bibliography

Michael Sullivan
The Birth of Landscape Painting in China
Routledge & Kegan Paul, London, 1962

9 Concert Champêtre

Oil painting by Giorgione, Italy. *c.* 1508

THE GREATEST PAINTERS of the Italian Renaissance seem either to have lived to an immense age or to have died young: Titian lived to nearly ninety-nine years, and Michelangelo to eighty-nine: Raphael died at thirty-seven, and Giorgione at possibly about thirty years. Yet Vasari, the intimate friend of the aged Michelangelo, calls Giorgione, with Leonardo da Vinci, the inventor of modern painting, that is, of the painting of the High Renaissance, to which all the painters cited belong. The originality of Leonardo, the senior of all these masters by over twenty years, is easily accepted: he was a universal genius; painting was only one, if the most important, of his many supreme talents, and though he finished only a small number of paintings, they rank among the greatest masterpieces in the history of art. The reputation of Giorgione is, however, more difficult to resolve: he was, perhaps, the first to paint directly from nature on to the canvas, and not to construct his compositions from carefully prepared preliminary drawings; and he was, perhaps, the first also to specialise in painting small pictures, intended for private collectors, of ambiguous subject matter which even his friends appear to have been not quite able to interpret. Moreover, when he died suddenly of the plague in 1510, he left a number of unfinished works which were to be completed by his followers, and his followers were painters as notable as his great contemporary Titian.

The *Concert Champêtre* is a case in point: the execution may be partly, or even wholly, Titian's, but the invention, the poetry and light of this pastoral scene, is certainly Giorgione's, and is indeed one of the great contributions he made to art. Experts may differ as to Giorgione's relative share in the actual execution; but surely Walter Pater was right, some eighty-five years ago, when he claimed that the favourite incidents of Giorgione's world were 'music, or the musical intervals in our existence, life itself conceived as a kind of listening – listening to music, to the reading of Bandello's novels, to the sound of water . . . When people are happy in this thirsty land, water will not be far off; and the presence of water – the well, or marble-rimmed pool, the drawing or pouring of water, as the woman pours it from a pitcher with her jewelled hand in the *Fête Champêtre* (that is, the present painting), listening perhaps to the cool sound as it falls, blent with the music of the pipes – is as characteristic, and almost as suggestive, as that of music itself'.

Giorgione's musicians have come to the end of one madrigal, and are resting before the next. The youths are talking about how they had played the last piece: one sees the conversation as a *post mortem*. The lute player seems to be, but is not, tuning up; his right hand is left poised as he discourses eagerly with his companion, who listens attentively. The seated girl has just sounded a note on her recorder, which she has lowered for a moment to join in the discussion; while the other girl, the singer apparently, has got up to fetch water for them all, but chiefly to refresh her own throat. Had Pater looked more closely, he would have seen that she was not pouring water away, but drawing water, and that the 'pipes' were momentarily silent – or very nearly silent, for evidently, too, the music they have just been making hangs in the air, has been heard from afar by the shepherd, and has dissolved into the quiet evening landscape.

If we suppose that Giorgione's *Concert Champêtre* was left unfinished on his early death in 1510, and that a large share of the handiwork was the young Titian's, Giorgione's invention can at least be placed with fair certainty at the end of the first decade of the sixteenth century, and that is a fact of some historical importance. In the fifteenth century, even in musical Venice, it is hard to find a painting in which music is so ingrained, or one in which art, to

It is strange that knowledge of the life of the artist, so highly regarded in his own century, should be so shrouded in mystery – a mystery as profound as that which surrounds the meaning of his own so poetic art. Master Zorzi (Venetian dialect for Giorgio) of Castelfranco, as he is named in the earliest reference to him, the inscription on the portrait of a lady in Vienna dated in 1506, was apparently brought up in Castelfranco, a town on the Venetian mainland. It is not known when he was born, but he could have been little more than thirty years of age when he died in 1510. He was a contemporary – possibly not even an older contemporary – and the peer in his life-time of his great compatriot Titian, who outlived him by sixty-six years.

One of the great original geniuses of European painting, his own contribution appears to have been a type of painting of problematic subject matter which depends so much for its meaning on the deep poetry of its atmosphere, and of which the *Concert Champêtre* is an outstanding example. Especially significant was the inspiration of this landscape of mood for the further development of landscape painting in Europe; Titian, and eventually the Venetian school in general, owed much to his first example; and in the seventeenth century, many a painter, like the great Poussin (Plate 13), sought inspiration from the poetry of Venetian landscape paintings.

9. CONCERT CHAMPÊTRE
The Louvre Museum, Paris

Giorgione. *Ca.* 1508.
Oil painting. 43¼ x 54¼ in.: 110 x 138 cm.

use Pater's memorable phrase, 'so constantly aspires to the condition of music, so completely realises this perfect identification of matter and form'. There are plenty of fifteenth-century artists who delight in the spectacle of musicians playing; Carpaccio, for instance, goes in for military bands, and drums thump and trumpets flare in half a dozen of his backgrounds; but they serve only to enhance that deep, withdrawn, melancholy silence which seems to be the abiding principle of his narrative style. In many an altarpiece, too, by the Bellini, Cima and lesser masters, charming children perform on mandolins, flageolets and rebecs at the foot of the Madonna's throne; but one feels that they are merely accomplishing a necessary ritual act and so cannot arouse much curiosity about the sounds they are so busily producing.

But with Giorgione – and one must pronounce the name as a symbol – all is changed, and nothing will be the same again. Perhaps it is that the art of music itself took a great leap forward in expressiveness at just this moment; and there are reasons for believing that this was the case. Perhaps the merely mechanical fact of the invention of printed music gave to music a new social dimension, rather as the invention of radio and television in our day has enormously encouraged the latent sensibility of a vast new public that until then had no notion of its own capacities and appetites. At this time, the time of transition from the fifteenth to the sixteenth century, Venice was the nerve centre of the great new movements and events in the field of music, and it was only to be expected that a Venetian artist should bear witness to these events. And it is hardly a coincidence that the agent for the change in the visual arts should have been one who, in addition to his profound inventiveness in his own profession as a painter, should have been renowned among his contemporaries as a supremely accomplished musician: Giorgione.

Roger Hinks †

Bibliography

Duncan Phillips and H. G. Dwight
The Leadership of Giorgione
American Federation of Arts,
Washington, 1937

10 The Mystery of Christ's Birth

Panel painting. From the Isenheim Altarpiece, by Matthias Grünewald, Germany. 1513–1515

THIS IS surely one of the most wondrous paintings in the whole of Christian art. As in a dream, all degrees of reality seem to be simultaneously present.

Leaving the curious Gothic temple on the left, we behold a simple domestic scene, the young mother with her child, a cradle, a wooden bath-tub and the humble chamber pot. Yet this group is not placed in the intimacy of a room, but in a walled garden with a mountainous landscape beyond. Indeed, both heaven and earth seem to be their abode, for above, in a splendour of light and colour, angels descend from the throne of God.

When we look back at the strange, visionary temple, we discover that here also the spheres merge. Plants grow out of the architectural ornament, and the little statues on their columns are in animated discussion with each other (Fig. 10a); the frontiers between art and nature, between fantasy and reality, the animate and inanimate, are fluid.

Fig. 10a. *Detail from* The Mystery of Christ's Birth – *an architectural ornament of the Temple.*

Until quite recently almost nothing was known of Grünewald apart from the existence of his one great masterpiece, the Isenheim Altarpiece, perhaps the most remarkable original artistic creation of its time. There is still no evidence for the name, Grünewald, which first appears over one hundred years after his death; contemporary documents, recently brought to light, refer to the master as Mathis Gothart Nithart.

Matthias was born at Würzburg probably between the years 1470 and 1480. By 1501 he had settled in Seligenstadt, near Aschaffenburg where his first important patron, the Archbishop of Mainz, had his residence. He died in 1528, the same year as his great German contemporary Dürer.

He was one of a number of great masters working at the time of the apogee of German painting, masters such as Dürer, Holbein and Altdorfer. As distinct from his great German contemporaries, he was apparently exclusively a painter – the others were masters also of engraving. If affected by the atmosphere of Humanism of his time, he was nevertheless exclusively a religious painter. He lived at a time of great spiritual disturbance, the time of the Reformation, of Luther (of whom he was to become an adherent), of the Peasants' War (1525); and his paintings are the most original and poignant expression of this atmosphere at the dawn of the New Age in Germany.

10. THE MYSTERY OF CHRIST'S BIRTH – from the Isenheim Altarpiece
Musée d'Unterlinden, Colmar, France

Grünewald. 1513-1515.
Panel painting. $104\frac{1}{2}$ x 101 in.: 265 x 256 cm.

Fig. 10b. *Detail from* The Mystery of Christ's Birth – *Angels in the Temple.*

What goes on inside the temple is unearthly and bewildering. A first impression is that of moths and butterflies hovering, fluttering in eager density around a light. They are angels in different colours, those in the background raising their hands in adoration, while in the foreground three larger and strangely hued angels perform a musical trio on fantastically shaped string-instruments (Fig. 10b). The light in their midst emanates from the halo surrounding the figure of a young girl who wears a crown, her face and hair bathed in the gold of the light (Fig. 10c).

Fig. 10c. *Detail from* The Mystery of Christ's Birth – *The Crowned Virgin in the Temple.*

The two parts of the painting are obviously interconnected. The crowned Virgin in the temple is looking at the Christ Child. Even more important is the figure of the angel in the foreground (Fig. 10d). He is not only larger but is above all more human than the angelic host inside the temple. He is kneeling before the Virgin and Child, his eyes fastened in adoration upon the group; it is obviously for them that he performs his music. To understand this musical offering we have to explain briefly the painting as a whole.

Note that the title, The Mystery of Christ's Birth, is ambivalent: it describes both an event and its religious significance, and the painting does the same. This ambivalence is characteristic of all works of Christian Art: they all seek to convey two things at once, the concrete event thought to have happened at a definite time and place and also its theological meaning which transcends time and place, rendering transparent whatever our eyes behold and impalpable whatever our hands seem to be able to grasp.

The wall surrounding the garden in which Mary is seated and the rose-bush are well-known symbols of her virginity. The domestic objects at her feet are not just the fragmentary furnishings of a nursery; they are there to remind us of the humility that made God descend from the throne of His majesty to become an infant in swaddling clothes. The delightful little flask of clear glass is another symbol (Fig. 10e): an ancient hymn calls Mary a 'spiritual vase', while a medieval song compares her purity to that of transparent glass. This flask stands on the threshold of the temple, significantly connecting both parts of the composition and providing a clue to the meaning of the representation on the left.

The most likely explanation of this scene is the legend according to which the Virgin before her marriage served in the temple where angels attended her. The temple itself is an image of the Virgin, since both are, as it were, the house of God. Here in the temple, the legend tells us, Mary beheld daily the vision of God, and in depicting Mary in the temple Christian artists sought to convey the splendour appropriate to Mary's dignity as a priestess and as a queen of heaven. Thus, on a statue of Mary in the temple her girdle bears an inscription from the Song of Songs (6, 9): 'Who is she that steps forth like the dawn of early light, beautiful like the moon, resplendent like the sun'. This passage may also be a clue to Grunewald's virgin in the temple, where above her head angels hold a crown, sceptre and globe, the traditional attributes of the heavenly queen.

Now that the main elements of the painting have been identified, we may attempt to interpret the meaning of the whole composition, which is unique. The first thing to recall is the simultaneous presence of different spheres of reality. Grünewald has deliberately stressed the difference between these realities. The Virgin and Child and the simple domestic objects are painted with great realism. In her humble posture and somewhat plain features she seems to be a young woman of the painter's own time. Immediately by the side of this domestic group, however, he places the dream vision of the mystical temple in order to recall who the young mother and child really are. This contrast between the two parts of the painting is deliberate and is meant to invoke that paradox which is the quintessence of the Christian faith: Christ is both God and the poorest of men.

Grünewald is the great dramatist of this paradox. The present painting is but the inside of an altarpiece. Upon the outside Grünewald painted his celebrated *Crucifixion* (Fig. 10f), where Christ's body appears maimed, tortured and covered with wounds, presenting this other mystery of the Christian faith, Christ's sacrifice for man's redemption, as a tragic paradox. The paradox of the mystery of Christ's Incarnation is not tragic but joyful,

Fig. 10d. *Detail from* The Mystery of Christ's Birth – *The Angel before the Temple.*

Fig. 10e. *Detail from* The Mystery of Christ's Birth – *Flask on the threshold of the Temple.*

Fig. 10f. *The Isenheim Altarpiece closed, showing* The Crucifixion.

but the tension is nevertheless present as in the *Crucifixion*. When we look at the figure of the angel in the foreground, one of the greatest and most characteristic creations of Grünewald's imagination, we feel this tension (Fig. 10d).

The theme of the Virgin and Child with music-making angels is not novel. Angels singing or playing musical instruments appear frequently behind or flanking the throne of the Virgin and Child (see Plate 7, Figs. 7b and 7c): Grünewald's Italian contemporaries often liked to place a single music-making angel at the feet of the Virgin. In all these cases the angels belong to her celestial court, and enhance her Majesty as they give voice to their adoration. In Grünewald's vision, however, the theme has become something quite different. We have already spoken of the relationship between the Virgin and angel; yet while this relationship is essential to the unity of the composition it is first of all one of contrast. The raptured expression on the angel's face as he kneels in adoration – mediator of our own emotions – contrasts as significantly with the calmness of the Virgin, as the down-to-earth humility of her appearance contrasts with the mysterious splendour of the temple. What really blends these contrasts into a whole is the music that the angel performs on his cello. This music, which seems to pervade the entire painting is obviously the angel's response to the vision he beholds. In this vision an extraordinary transformation takes place before our eyes: the simple mother appears transfigured into the heavenly priestess and queen as the reality that religion has revealed to the believer. The angel's music gives voice to this ecstatic experience. The history of art knows no other figure of a musician so enraptured because no other painter has conveyed as music man's response to ultimate reality.

Otto von Simson

Bibliography

J. K. Huysmans and E. Ruhmer
Grünewald Paintings
Phaidon Press, London, 1958

H. von Einem
Die Menschwerdung Christi
in Arbeitsgemeinschaft für Forschung des Landes Nordrhein-Westfalen, Geisteswissenschaften, 55, Cologne, 1955

11 A Festive Scene

Page from an illuminated manuscript, by Maqsud, Iran. Mid 16th century

THIS PAINTING records how in olden times the people of Persia (Iran) enjoyed music and dancing. It is one of the illustrations to a poem by the celebrated Jami, one of the last classical poets of Persia. The poem itself which accompanies the illumination was penned in the fine handwriting of the famous calligrapher Ali al-Husayni of Herat, and was illustrated by various artists, including some of the most renowned of the time such as Maqsud and Qasim Ali. Authorities agree that the calligraphy and illustra-

Fig. 11. Barbud playing before King Khosru. *Miniature by Mirza Ali from the Khamseh of Nizami, Iran.* 1539–43.

11. A FESTIVE SCENE
Imperial Museum, Teheran

Maqsud. Mid 16th century.
A page from an illuminated manuscript.

tions belong to the middle of the sixteenth century and are typical of the so-called Shiraz School, which is characterised by its imaginative adaptation of traditional patterns and the excellence of its craftsmanship.

The artist who has with so much feeling conveyed to us in this painting the atmosphere of this festive occasion, the charming gaiety of the music and dance which he has made to flow and weave over the surface of his page, does not appear to have recorded his name on this particular illustration, but the similarity in style with some other illustrations in the manuscript convincingly points to Maqsud as the artist, the able pupil of the great master of Persian painting, Bihzad.

The scene the artist has portrayed so vividly for us suggests, like the majority of Persian illuminations, that of a dreamland, with its flowers, its elegance and gaiety, its people engaged in festivity in the midst of Nature, 'on an early morning in spring' – a theme and setting so often sung by the poets of Persia.

If depth is indicated by the flattened-out perspective of the enclosure, the artist relies essentially on surface pattern. The more distant figures are placed higher on the page, but we are not intended to be viewing the scene from above. The central figure of this spiral of dancers and onlookers – the man playing the 'lute' who seems to lead the music – in no way dominates the composition. The movement is both initiated by this figure and returns to it, and is also carried upwards by the upraised hands of the dancers in the background and by the branches of the trees. Our eyes and attention, like the music, are left to wander over the whole surface of the page, through the whole of this dreamland created by the painter, with the help of the minute detail – the blossom on the trees, the costumes, the different instruments, the elegant lines of the figures. The central figure is playing upon the *al-ud*, a string instrument resembling the lute and still a fairly popular instrument in Persia, accompanied by the *chang*, an instrument resembling the harp, held by the woman on the left, and the tambourine, held by the woman to her right. The artist has created each small detail with such care and delicacy that he captivates our imagination. The figures too, even the farthest away from us, are drawn with the same clarity. The pattern is so integrated and the spirit so sustained that with all the wealth of detail nothing falls apart. On the left, even the horse is caught up by the spirit of the music and dance. The two men, possibly attendants, on the farthest side of the enclosure, one apparently holding a basket of fruit, are similarly absorbed in the festivity they are witnessing. On the left, a boy seems to be clapping his hands to the music. The painter has, above all, captured effectively the rhythmic movements of the hands and feet of the circle of dancing girls.

In spite of the romantic mood of the scene, it is not divorced from reality. Indeed, the artist is depicting an everyday scene, one which even today is not uncommon in Persia; but he has depicted it in a style that transforms it into a magical world of delightful, natural detail and fine, delicate lines and colours, creating so vividly this atmosphere of festivity, of music and song, in whose exquisite mood we may participate and lose ourselves like these musicians and dancers of four hundred years ago.

Fakhir Hussain

Bibliography

Basil Gray
Persian painting from miniatures of 13th–16th centuries
Batsford, London, 1947

H. Pinder-Wilson
Persian Painting of the 15th century
The Faber Gallery of Oriental Art,
Faber & Faber, London, 1958

12 Music in a Spring Garden

Detail from an illuminated scroll, by Tosa Mitsunori, Japan. *c.* 1630

A WOODEN PAVILION, with its lacquered pillars and terraces, built on the edge of a lake, whose waters come right up to the courtyard and beat gently against the rocks seen in the right foreground of the picture, is depicted with great delicacy. A cherry-tree in blossom rises up to the height of the terrace where the Empress Akikononu and a lady-in-waiting sit behind fine screens listening to the music of a flute played by one of the men seen to the right of the terrace. A moon rises through the mist and clouds surrounding the building.

This is one of the illustrations to the great Japanese medieval novel, *The Tale of Genji*, by the Lady Murasaki, written about 1001–1015. The painting, executed in ink, illustrates an incident from *The Butterflies*, a chapter devoted to a spring excursion by the ladies of the court, who on this occasion went by boat from one pavilion to another to look at the spring gardens and to listen to music.

> Towards the end of the third month, when out in the country the orchards were no longer at their best and the song of the wild birds had lost its freshness, Murasaki's Spring Garden seemed only to become every day more enchanting. The little wood on the hill beyond the lake, the bridge that joined the two islands, the mossy banks that seemed to grow greener not every day but every hour – could anything have looked more tempting? 'If only one could get there!' sighed the young people of the household; and at last Genji decided that there must be boats on the lake . . . They discovered to their delight that the shape of every little ledge and crag of stone had been so carefully devised as if a painter had traced them with his brush. Here and there in the distance the topmost boughs of an orchard showed above the mist, so heavily laden with blossom that it looked as though a bright carpet were spread in mid-air . . .
>
> So captivated were they by this novel experience that they had soon lost all sense of whither they were faring or whence they had come. It was indeed as though the waters had cast a spell of forgetfulness upon their hearts . . .
>
> It seemed a pity that darkness should be allowed to interfere with these pleasures, and when night came on, a move was made to the courtyard in front of the palace. Here flares were lit, and on the mossy lawn at the feet of the Great Steps not only musicians but also various visitors from the Court and friends of the family performed on wind and string, while picked teachers of the flute gave a display in the 'double mode'. Then all the zitherns and lutes belonging to the different members of the household were brought out onto the steps and carefully tuned to the same pitch. A grand concert followed, the piece 'Was ever such a day?' being performed with admirable effect. Even the grooms and labourers who were loitering amid the serried ranks of coaches drawn up outside the great gates, little as they cared for such things, on this occasion pricked up their ears and were soon listening with lips parted in wonder and delight. For it was indeed impossible that the strange shrill descants of the 'Spring mode', enhanced as they were by the unusual beauty of the night, should not move the most impercipient of human creatures.
>
> The concert continued until dawn. As a return-tune, 'Gay Springtide Pleasures' was added to the programme, and Prince Sochi-no-Miya carried the vocal music back very pleasantly to the 'common mode' by singing 'Green Willows' in the words of which Genji also joined.
>
> Already the morning birds were clamouring in a lusty chorus to which, from behind the curtains, the Empress Akikononu listened . . .

The description in the novel has a romantic elegance, ephemeral as the spring itself. The painting expresses all this, and expresses too the nostalgic melancholy brought out by the fragile notes of the flutes: the two ladies have their heads bent slightly in an attitude of gentle sadness. The artist has chosen from all the technical means at his disposal those elements which would enable him to express the essential emotions caused by such a scene: the use of fine ink lines, the lack of vivid colour – apart from the ink-black there are

For scroll paintings see note to Plate 8. Scroll painting originated in China and was imported into Japan in the 8th or 9th century. The important development of the art in Japan took place in the 12th to 14th century.

Tosa Mitsunori (1563–1638) was a member of a family of noted artists. The so-called Tosa School of painting, or Tosa style, is characterised by the delicate line-work favoured at the court. The illustration of the Japanese classics formed an important part of the Tosa tradition, *The Tale of Genji* occuring most frequently. Tosa Mitsunori's illustration to the tales is probably the finest.

The authoress of *The Tale of Genji*, Lady Murasaki (Murasaki Shikibu), was born about 978. On the death of her husband she entered the service of the Empress Akiko. *The Tale of Genji* was probably begun in 1001, and was finished about 1015 to 1020.

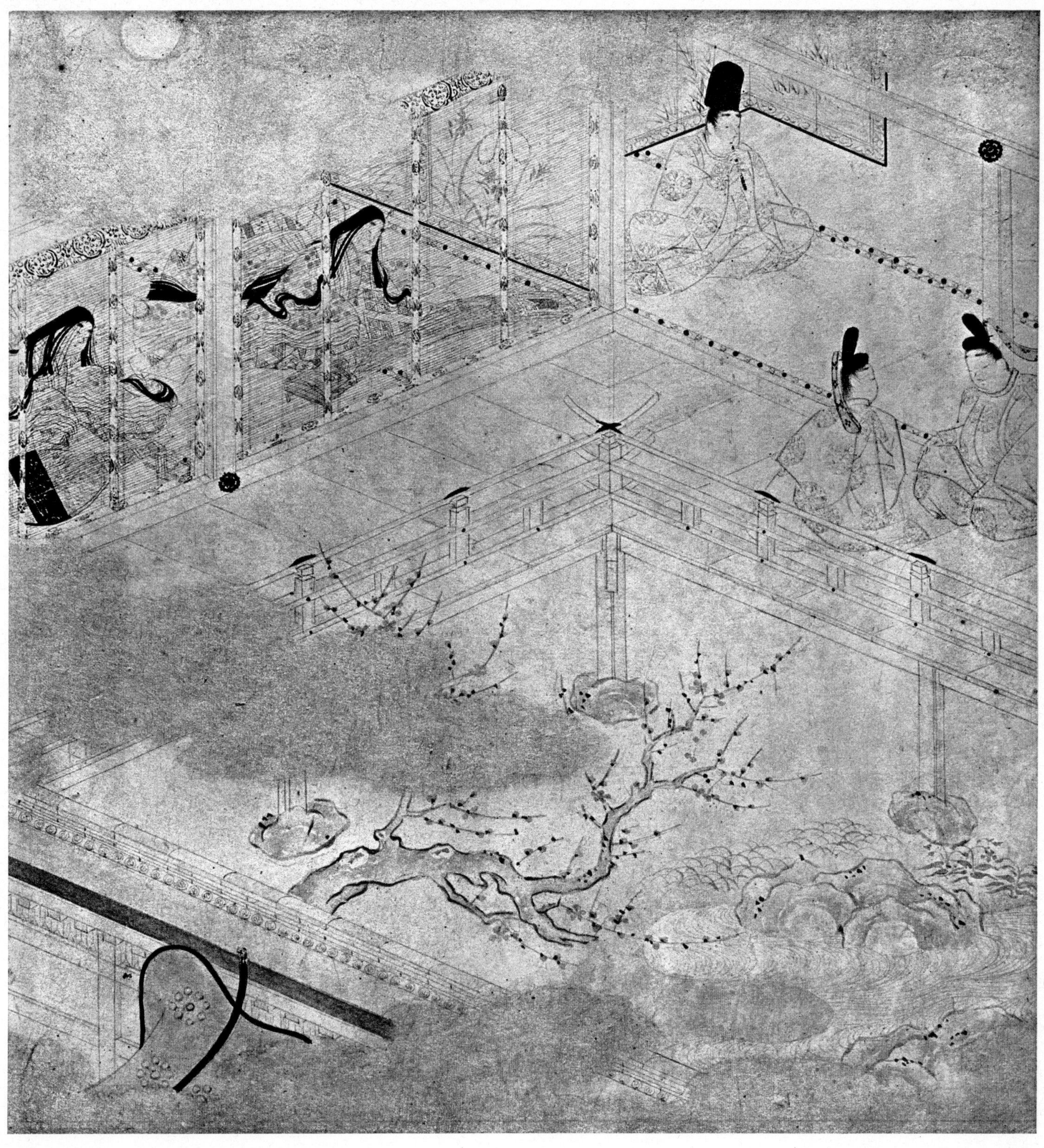

12. MUSIC IN A SPRING GARDEN
Freer Gallery of Art, Washington, USA

Tosa Mitsunori. *Ca.* 1630.
From a Japanese scroll painting. 5⅞ x 5⅜ in.: 15 x 14 cm.

Fig. 12. *Detail from* Music in a Spring Garden – *Flute Player and Listener.*

only touches of gold in the painting – are expressive of the delicate music of the picture.

One of the outstanding characteristics of traditional Japanese music is perhaps the fact that it exists primarily in combination with poems, literature or dramatic works. Purely instrumental orchestral music was imported around the sixth or seventh century from Korea, China, Indo-China and India to become the court music called *Gagaku*. It was this kind of music that the court ladies in *The Tale of Genji* listened to on that spring night. The flute played by the man sitting on the terrace is in reality a kind of oboe, which with various types of flute were used in Gagaku music. Apart from this Gagaku music, the later development of traditional Japanese music – Noli music, Kabuki music, ballads with lute accompaniment, etc. – can be said to be inseparable from the text which it underlines and ornaments: it tries to enhance each word, and to express the joys and sorrows of the human heart contained in the words. In this painting the artist has used his brush to reveal the somewhat fragile elegance of ancient court life.

Morikuni Toda

Bibliography

For the text of 'The Tale of Genji':
Arthur Waley (trans.)
The Tale of Genji
Allen & Unwin, London, 1925

R. T. Paine and A. Soper
The Art and Architecture of Japan
Pelican History of Art
Penguin Books, Harmondsworth, 1955

13 Orpheus and Eurydice

Oil painting by Nicolas Poussin, France. *c.* 1650

NO OTHER MYTH of Greek antiquity pays a more moving tribute to the power of music than that of Orpheus. His song, we are told, could charm wild beasts, the trees and the mountains, and finally even the dread deities of the underworld, the dwelling place of the dead. For, so the legend has it, while Orpheus was singing, his bride Eurydice was bitten by a snake and died, and so heart-rending was the lament of Orpheus over his beloved that it finally moved even the rulers of the dead. They gave him permission to bring Eurydice back to the world if during the long, anguished ascent he would refrain from turning back to look upon her. However, Orpheus, 'eager for sight of her, turned back his longing eyes', and Eurydice was taken from him for ever.

This myth is the subject of one of the most perfect paintings of Poussin, the great French painter of the seventeenth century. It is not difficult to recognise the moment chosen. Orpheus is seated in the foreground in the shadow of a great tree, absorbed by his song which he accompanies on his lyre. Two maidens seated in front of him are spell-bound by his voice; but the centre of the stage is occupied by a strange figure which seems to have appeared from nowhere. We do not know if he listens to the divine singer; more likely he is the harbinger of some portent. Above all he stands between Orpheus and Eurydice, thus preventing Orpheus from perceiving that she is in danger, and from coming to her rescue. For Eurydice is about to be bitten by a snake, which is visible to her left, and from which she is trying to flee.

The standing figure has long remained enigmatic but its recent identification with Hymen seems plausible for Hymen appears in the literary source which Poussin used, the *Metamorphoses* by the Roman poet Ovid. 'Thence through the boundless air Hymen, clad in a saffron mantle, departed and took his way to the country of Ciconians, and was summoned by the voice of Orpheus, though all in vain. He was present, it is true; but he brought

Orpheus was a legendary musician born in Thrace, where Greece and the Mediterranean merge with the Balkan mountains and Central Europe. In antiquity his home lay on the northern boundaries of Greek civilization, a mysterious region where the god Dionysus held sway (see Plate 2). Orpheus was the singer of songs so potent that the Maenads, the ecstatic Thracian women who worshipped Dionysus, tore him to pieces. His severed head, it is said, floated away singing to the island of Lesbos. Such is the mythical power of music, the mythical fate of musicians. An English poem, contemporary with Poussin, gives us an idea of the fascination that the Orpheus myth had on European intellectuals of that age:

Orpheus with his Lute made trees,
And the Mountaine tops that freeze,
Bow themselves when he did sing.
To his Musicke, Plants and Flowers
Ever sprung; as Sunne and Showers,
There had made a lasting Spring.
Everything that heard him play,
Even the Billowes on the Sea,
Hung their heads, and then lay by.
In sweete Musicke is such Art,
Killing care, and griefe of heart,
Fall asleepe, or hearing die.
(Fletcher, in '*Henry VIII*')

Fig. 13. *Detail from* Orpheus and Eurydice.

13. ORPHEUS AND EURYDICE — Poussin. *Ca.* 1650.
The Louvre Museum, Paris — Oil painting. $48\frac{3}{4}$ x $78\frac{3}{4}$ in.: 124 x 200 cm.

Poussin, French painter, born Les Andelys, Normandy, *c.* 1594; settled Rome *c.* 1624; died Rome 1665. His painting was inspired especially by the literature and art of antiquity. One of the most learned of European painters in an age when an artist was expected to be a mythographer, he owed a great deal to the Latin poets such as Ovid and Virgil.

In particular, he was deeply interested in the musical modes, and equated them to the tone of his own paintings. The seventeenth-century curiosity about the spiritual and moral analogies of the various modes is revealed in the discourse of a contemporary lutenist.

Poussin visited Venice early in his career, when he came into contact with the works of the great sixteenth-century painter Titian, and he certainly derived inspiration from the Venetian landscapes of 'mood' of which Giorgione (see Plate 9) and Titian were the pioneers. His preoccupation with landscape as an expression of man's experience was an entirely new notion in Italy – and especially in Rome – in the seventeenth-century, where it was considered that 'the proper study of mankind was man'. In northern Europe this love of nature remains a characteristic trait. Poussin gave himself more and more to a study of landscape, to that communion with nature which comes so naturally to Asian people.

R.H.

Bibliography

A. F. Blunt
Art and Architecture of France
Pelican History of Art
Penguin Books, Harmondsworth, 1953

André Chastel
Nicolas Poussin
Editions du CNRS, Paris, 1961

Ovid, *Metamorphoses*
trans. Frank J. Miller and
W. Heinemann
Harvard University Press, 1951–2

W. Friedländer
Hymenaea
in *De Artibus Opuscula, XL – Essays in honour of Erwin Panofsky*
ed. Millard Meiss
New York University Press, 1961

neither the hallowed words, nor joyous faces, nor lucky omens. The torch also which he held kept sputtering and filled the eyes with smoke, nor would it catch fire for any brandishing' (hence, perhaps, the smoking castle in the background, the scene of the wedding feast). 'The outcome of the wedding was worse than the beginning, for while the bride was strolling through the grass with a group of naiads in attendance, she fell dead, smitten in the ankle by a serpent's tooth'.

In Ovid's account Hymen, normally the divine patron of weddings, appears in an ominous role; to the bride-groom, Orpheus, he brings 'neither joyous faces nor lucky omens'. Ovid, of course, knew ancient mythology better than Poussin, and in his brief description of Hymen there may even echo undertones that connect the ancient myth of Hymen with early death, as incidentally they connect him with the spirit of music. Poussin could not know this, but in reading the apparently simple and short account by Ovid he seems to have intuitively grasped the ancient meaning of the Orpheus myth in which Hymen is not the conventional wedding guest but rather the messenger of doom.

The mythological group in Poussin's painting forms but a small part of the composition, but it is unquestionably the centre, and the clue to our understanding of the whole. In the last years of his life Poussin became more and more preoccupied with landscape as a symbol of the most solemn moments of man's experience. Poussin is one of the greatest landscape painters of the Western tradition, but his landscapes are attuned to a mood of philosophic humanism, and provide the setting for a moral drama. Though reduced in physical scale, man always remains in the centre of Poussin's landscapes. The mountains, woods, rivers and cities, and even the skies themselves, are witness to the human or heroic destiny in question. To a mind that so conceived the relationship of man to nature, the fable of Orpheus would naturally be congenial; and in fact Poussin's picture, painted around 1650, is one of his masterpieces. As indicated, he has chosen the moment just before the tragic climax. Orpheus is not yet aware that Eurydice will die, and she herself is still alive. There is a strange contrast between the musician and his serene rapture and the figure of Hymen that appears to beckon Orpheus silently but unheeded.

All this is set in a landscape of varied harmony, which is however assailed by the powers of darkness. The foreground is cast in deep shadows that seem to rise like a dark tide and begin to envelop the figures. At the same time, sombre clouds begin to overcast the luminosity of the sky. These movements are almost imperceptible, and a great stillness pervades the landscape. There is little doubt that Poussin wished to convey the silent attention of nature to Orpheus' music. Does not Nature hold her breath to listen? Not a leaf stirs on the trees, not a ripple on the water, and even the clouds halt momentarily.

Poussin's art is often permeated by the knowledge of death. Twice he depicted this knowledge in a particularly poignant way. Shepherds in an idyllic setting venture innocently upon a sarcophagus with an inscription that reminds them that death is present even here. It is characteristically the same thought that Poussin chose for his representation of Orpheus and Eurydice. His painting is concerned with the undying splendour of music, we might say, on the very brink of death. The two forces are equipoised: Orpheus' music cannot save Eurydice; but the realm of death seems to be outside the charmed circle of the celestial song.

Roger Hinks †

(*The Editors have completed this text which remained unfinished at the time of Roger Hinks' death.*)

14 David playing before Saul

Oil painting by Rembrandt, Holland. *c.* **1657**

THE BLACK-BEARDED, melancholy Saul listens to the playing of the harp. He sits, his head covered with his heavy turban and crown, his robes agleam with the sombre splendour of the oriental ruler as Europeans pictured them some three hundred years ago. His right hand, noble and nervous, rests lightly against the javelin in his arm. His large form appears to be seated rather high, possibly upon a throne or dais. The young David, playing on his harp, appears to be seated or kneeling much below him, and in comparison he is very small. The two are alone with the rise and fall of the music conjured forth by the young musician. There is no indication of a setting, but we might imagine this to be the interior of a royal tent. The light enters from the foreground, sparingly and uncertainly, apparently through a rather narrow gap, picking out, with a strange and wonderful gleam, a form here and there, and leaving the rest in darkness.

The space above the boy is obscure and almost void. It has been suggested that this replaces part of the canvas that at one time had been cut away, as was the case with many of Rembrandt's paintings. However that may be, nothing could add to the painting in terms either of its composition or its content.

'Meanwhile the Lord's spirit passed away from Saul; instead, at the Lord's bidding, an evil mood came over him that gave him no rest. God sends thee an evil mood, his servants told him, to disquiet thee. We are thy servants, waiting on our Lord's bidding; shall we go and find some skilful player of the harp, to relieve thee, when God visits thee with this evil mood, by his music? Yes, answered Saul, find one who can play the harp well, and bring him to me. And here one of his servants offered advice; Stay, I myself have such a man, a skilful player indeed, a son of Jesse the Bethlehemite; He is sturdy besides, and a tried warrior, well-spoken and personable, and the Lord is with him. Thereupon a message went out from Saul to Jesse. There is a son of thine, David, that looks after thy sheep; send him to me. And Jesse loaded an ass with bread, and a flagon of wine, and a kid, and sent these by David as a present to Saul. Thus it was that David met Saul and entered his service; and became his armour-bearer, so well Saul loved him. Let David remain here in attendance on me, Saul told Jesse; and I like him well. And whenever Saul was taken with the evil mood of his, David would fetch the harp, and play; whereupon Saul was comforted and felt easier, till at last the evil mood left him'. (1 Samuel, 16, xiv–xxiii)

Yet the rapport between the two men was darkly ambiguous. Saul is one of the tragic figures of the Old Testament, and his relationship with David is fraught with drama. We are not told why the spirit of God passed from him and went into David – the Bible does not mention any guilt on Saul's part that may have caused it – but Saul knows that the Divine favour is with David who will inherit the kingdom from him, and the dark and evil moods that take possession of him are certainly connected with this knowledge. Twice while David was playing before him, Saul sought to kill him by throwing the javelin at him. After many attempts to take David's life, none successful, and all the more humiliating for Saul in the knowledge that more than once David had spared his life when he had him at his mercy, Saul was finally to be defeated by David and to die in battle.

Throughout Christian tradition, Saul appears as the dark shadow of David. The Middle Ages depicted David in the glory of God's anointed, that made him the example of every king and as the ancestor of Christ, while Saul appeared defeated beneath his feet. However, the other, affectionate relation-

Rembrandt Harmensz. van Rijn, Dutch painter, engraver and draughtsman, was born at Leyden, 1606, settled in Amsterdam in 1631 or 1632, where by the 1640's he had already attained universal fame in Europe and a certain material success; he died in Amsterdam in 1669, after some two decades of material hardship and personal tragedies. His early acclaim depended in large part on his powers as a portrait painter and upon his new interpretation of Biblical stories; the spiritual content of his later paintings, however, was not understood by his former patrons and his popularity rapidly declined. One of the few really outstanding original geniuses of painting in Europe, he essayed every type of subject (the portrait, landscape, still-life, stories of the Bible, myth and history) giving to all a deep spiritual interpretation. He developed a style of immense originality, freedom and power, which relied especially on an individual use of colour and light, and he remains one of the great colourists in European painting. Also one of the few really great graphic artists of Europe, the same qualities as in his paintings appear in his drawings, in which he essayed almost every technique, and in his etchings, and in both spheres his output was prodigious.

14. DAVID PLAYING BEFORE SAUL
The Mauritshuis, The Hague, Netherlands

Rembrandt. *Ca.* 1657.
Oil painting. $51\frac{1}{4}$ x $64\frac{1}{2}$ in.: 130 x 164 cm.

Fig. 14. David playing before Saul *by Rembrandt. c.*1631.

ship between the two, that of the aging king finding consolation in his darkest moods by listening to the youth playing on his harp, was not forgotten. This scene was often recalled in order to point out the beneficial effects of music. There was harmony of the soul, philosophers taught, corresponding to the harmonies of music, and when the soul was in the turmoil of despair, its peace could be restored by the healing powers of music.

Rembrandt has given expression to this reality of music; the musical chords he renders visible seem to span, but not reconcile, the deep and ominous tension between the two human figures.

The tune that David's nimble fingers call forth from the gleaming strings of his harp seems to rise in golden ripples, and to play even upon Saul's garment. Yet the painting remains cast in darkness. Saul lifts the curtain to his eye, as if furtively to wipe away a tear. But the disturbing expression on his face leaves us apprehensive – does he wish to conceal his thoughts?

Rembrandt, who knew the Bible intimately and demanded of his pupils the same knowledge, knew that the people for whom he painted would also recognize the javelin in Saul's hand as the deadly weapon that he had suddenly hurled at David.

Whatever the location and function of the curtain may be, pictorially it creates a great chasm of darkness between the two protagonists, Saul and David. The expression on David's face also makes us ponder. Is he entirely absorbed in his playing? Or is a hidden vigilance aware of the fearful presence of the king whose murderous weapon, the Bible tells us, he evaded only by jumping aside with lightning speed?

Many years before, when still a young man, Rembrandt had treated the same theme (Fig. 14). The main elements of the present composition are already there in the earlier work: the disparity in size of the two actors, the play of light and shadow, the oriental splendour of Saul's attire, the curtain, the javelin and of course the harp. Yet the difference between the two paintings is immense. The young Rembrandt concentrates everything in one moment of suspense. There is no doubt that this Saul is about to hurl the javelin. We are unable to turn our eyes from the towering menace of that figure, from that shifty, merciless face, that almost insane stare fixed upon its victim, and that fist gripping the weapon (note the contrast with Saul's noble and almost fragile hand in the later painting).

What interested Rembrandt in his first treatment of the theme of Saul and David was a vision of tyrannical power, whose glare is so fearfully present among the deep, silent shadows of the tent – the power to overwhelm the helpless victim. It was this interpretation of Biblical subjects that made the young Rembrandt famous among his fellow citizens who eagerly bought his pictures. To us, his sense of high drama seems somewhat exaggerated, but to his contemporaries it was something which both excited and shocked them: no artist before him had used light to such dramatic effect.

In the later painting light is again handled as only Rembrandt knew how to handle it. Indeed, his dramatic use of light has become much more subtle and sensitive, producing an effect almost sublime and attuned to an entirely new and a more profound understanding of what passed between David and Saul. Saul no longer dominates the composition, is no longer in control of himself or ready for treacherous and murderous action. He is overcome by deep emotion, and his relationship to David is not that of the hunter to his prey but more complex and infinitely more human. When we compare the two paintings the secret of the later composition begins to emerge. This secret is the presence of an invisible third protagonist, which unites Saul and David together, paralysing Saul's arm and overwhelming his heart. This third element is the power of music, invisible yet the only true actor in the drama, because the minds of Saul and David are visibly transformed by its spell.

Above all, the painting is an uncanny evocation of music – more precisely, of music's power over man's soul. The contrast between the two human beings, the secret distance that separates them, could hardly be greater. The deep and splendid obscurity of the curtain separates them like a chasm. At the same time, however, this chasm is bridged, and the disparities are reconciled, by the music, which is taken up by the attitude of the musician and the curved line of the harp to lead us to the figure of Saul, which appears like a great and gleaming crescent, open, all-responsive, to the gentle magic of the tune. Rembrandt seems to have chosen these two antagonistic characters, each with his thoughts secretly divided, only to convey to us, in what at first glance appears the most disjointed among his great compositions, the soothing power of musical harmony.

Otto von Simson

Bibliography

Jakob Rosenberg
Rembrandt
Harvard University Press, Cambridge, Mass., 1948

Focillon and Goldschneider
Rembrandt
Phaidon Press, London, 1960

15 Kakubha Ragini

Illustration from a Ragamala series, Central India. *c.* **1660**

THIS PAINTING belongs to a series called the Ragamala Miniatures, which represent in visual terms the poetic description of a *Raga*, or Indian musical 'mode'; and if we abandon ourselves without resistance to the aesthetic emotion which emanates from the picture it may seem that the emotion is also one of a musical order which gradually envelops us.

The poem which accompanied the *Kakubha Ragini* describes a woman of startling beauty, who, tortured by separation from the man she loves, walks alone through the forest. The scene in this picture is highly formalised, yet the overall impression is one of abundance; luxurious vegetation bursts through the formalisation in an explosion of colour – green, red, blue.

The girl, adorned with jewels, stands exactly in the centre of the scene against a flame-coloured background; on either side, her figure is flanked by two tall trees with a small bush between them, strong and important elements in the design. She walks on the top of a bank which slopes down to a lotus pond in the lower right foreground of the picture. These elements convey a sense of movement, making us realise that she moves from the left to the right. The turn of her head and the two small bushes and half a tree on the left seem to push the figure of the girl to the right. The descending curve of the embankment and the rising curve of the pond and its sandy shore towards the path above make us experience the same sense of motion. There is no indication of depth or light; the trees are stacked together one behind the other much as playing cards. Through the trees and behind the burning colour surrounding the girl are indications of rocky hills. In the left background a banana tree shows its soft broad leaves, while beside it is a palm tree on which a bird seems to be sitting. Birds fly amidst this lyrical profusion which is rendered in delicate detail and vivid colour. The same delicacy of detail is used for the cranes, the ripples on the water and the lotus flowers in the pond. The branches of the tree to the right and of some of the bushes are curiously depicted, for they too look like birds in flight, and again these elements give us a further sense of movement.

The girl is indeed going away from the left, but she goes sadly and reluctantly; the turning of the head tells us that only her body moves while her mind is with her lover from whom she has been separated. The two peacocks who look up to her sympathetically are symbols of lovers, and the two garlands she holds in each hand are similar symbols, just as the colour of passion that surrounds her figure is a symbol of her violent emotion.

The possible correspondence between the arts and a certain mysterious relationship between music and painting is not specifically Indian, but no-one has gone so far as the Indian in its comprehension. The Sanskrit word *Sangita* signifying music embraces all three notions of vocal and instrumental music and the dance. It is, therefore, not surprising that it was in India that this garland of miniatures, the Ragamala, was born, in which music, poetry and painting are brought together.

'Towards the beginning of the seventeenth century there grew up in India a type of painting for which no exact parallels exist in the West – poetry, painting and music were brought into a new relationship. Through the verbal imagery of a poem, the musical form was given more precise expression, while in its turn, the picture made even clearer the interpretation attempted in the poem.'

These Ragamala paintings, however, on which are often inscribed the name and descriptive verse of the Ragas or Raginies (the feminine equivalents) which they illustrate, are not to be taken as visual representations of the musical 'mode', but rather as the visualisation of the emotional and aesthetic

Ragas and Raginies are the melodic structures of Indian classical music. The word Raga derives from the Sanskrit 'Ranja' ('to please'). While Raga and Ragini are the masculine and feminine derivatives, it is doubtful if masculine and feminine qualities can be ascribed to them. Each Raga must have a minimum of five notes, and distinct features and characters determined by: (1) the ascending and descending series of notes, that is, the number of notes and the order in which they are taken while ascending and descending in the octave; (2) the prominence of certain notes in relation to other notes in the Raga; (3) special melodic procedures peculiar to the Raga.

A Raga also has a definite time of the day when it is sung or played; dawn, midday, evening (not any evening but an evening in spring 'full of gaiety and love', or an evening during the monsoon rains). The convention is still followed in the Northern or Hindustani system of music, whereas in the Southern or Karnatski system it is largely disregarded. In the North the repertoire consists of about 125 to 150 Ragas; in the South the number is greater. New Ragas as well as new compositions in old Ragas are constantly added.

Based on notes by G.S.M.

Legend and myth ascribe the origin of Indian music to a divine source: five Ragas are born of the five faces of Shiva when he dances; the sixth is born from Shiva's wife Parvati: and the Raginies are born out of the God Brahma. Rhythm itself was born from Shiva. The names of the Ragas and Raginies have various origins, deriving from the names of flowers or birds, or from geographical or tribal names. According to Gangoly the name 'Kakubha' (the title of the present painting) probably came from a village well-known as a centre of culture during the Gupta Period (4th–6th century AD).

It is not known precisely when the first Ragamala were painted. Most date from the seventeenth century, and many belong to the Rajput School of painting. The decadence of the Ragamala miniatures began in the nineteenth century.

Though the conception of the Raga, in all its complexity and refinement, seems specifically Indian, there are many parallels in other parts of the world: in Ancient Greece, where an

15. KAKUBHA RAGINI – from a Ragamala Series
Victoria & Albert Museum, London

Central India. *Ca.* 1660.
Miniature painting. 9½ x 7½ in.: 24 x 19 cm.

ethical character was ascribed to different musical modes (Plate 2); in China, where again we find a correspondence between musical terms and the seasons; in Japan, the musical modes, influenced by the Indian Raga, were also used for specific seasons or occasions (Plate 12); in Syria and Turkey, the 'Maquam' obey the same laws as the Raga and are similarly considered to possess a spiritual power. Part of the importance of the 'Maquam' was the sentiment evoked in the listener; and again certain of the 'Maquam' belonged to certain hours of the day. In Egypt, the Najma; in Tunisia, the Taba; and in Algeria, the Sang, reveal the same conception.

Europeans too have considered the possible correspondence between the different arts, and have sensed at times a certain mysterious relationship between music and painting. The French painter Delacroix explains, in his *Journal*, a pictorial problem by saying, 'it is harmony and its combinations adapted to one song, it is musical tendency . . .'. For Gauguin, colour and music were of the same nature, both 'vibrating'; for the poet Baudelaire, 'perfumes, colours and sounds respond'; and Rimbaud's famous sonnet reads, 'A, black; E, white; R, red; U, green; O, blue'.

Lilian Lassen

Bibliography

H. J. Stooke and K. Khandalawala
The Laud Ragamala Miniatures
Bruno Cassirer, Oxford, 1953

O. G. Gangoly
Masterpieces of Rajput Painting
Calcutta, 1927

experience which the music gives; that is, they are concerned with its appreciation or listening.

The Indian classical arts, visual and aural, traditionally perform a common aesthetic function: they evoke in the spectator or listener a mood, flavour, or *rasa*. This is so whatever other function they may perform, and it is in its achievement that they arrive at their highest attainment and significance. For the work of art is not considered in the abstract, but in association with the audience to whom it is addressed. Music, for example, does not exist apart from the listener: 'all music is what awakes in you when you are reminded of it by the instruments' (Dasharupa, IV, 45). Considered in this light, Indian painting and sculpture depict two aspects of music, one dealing with its performance (see Plate 3), and the other with its appreciation or listening. It is with this latter aspect that we are concerned here.

The understanding of what happens when listening to music is complex and requires some knowledge of the Indian theory of aesthetics. This theory, known as the Theory of Rasa, was first formulated in Bharata's *Natya-Shastra*, around the third to fifth century AD. It establishes man and his fundamental emotional states or 'passions' at the centre of artistic activity. These fundamental and permanent emotions – love, sorrow, peace, fear, terror, heroism, disgust, wonder and ridicule – become transmuted into aesthetic emotions or *rasas*, through a magical process, as it were, which involves the quality of the work of art as well as the ability of the man who enjoys it. These *rasas*, evoked only in the 'right' spectator, the 'right' listener, by which is meant the sympathetic (Sarhydaya) audience, make possible an extra-ordinary experience. The listener, in the case of music for example, is in the midst of the drama of life, but being an uninvolved participant experiences its full passion in a state of 'unobstructed consciousness', without being personally torn by it. He is like the traditional lotus leaf, untouched by the surrounding water. His experience is also ecstatic, approaching the experience of the saint; *rasa* then fills him 'as a perfume fills a room', or burns in him like 'fire burns in dry wood'. It is this aspect of listening which the Ragamala paintings attempt to stress, depicting the erotic, heroic and sublime themes, the themes most commonly treated in Indian music.

In this painting almost everything is a symbol – it is like a language which in this case speaks to the initiated spectator or *rasika* (one who experiences *rasa*) of love, separation and longing, and when the *Kakubha Ragini* is played or sung it should ideally evoke in the listener the same emotions as the painting evokes by visual means.

This Theory of Rasa informs the whole intention and conception of the Ragamala Miniatures which are directed to man as listener, or *rasika*, who receives from music not only sensuous pleasure and intellectual satisfaction, but also an extended awareness, freeing him from the limitations of his personal self and exposing him to the experience of an impersonal, universal but human reality. This experience is not new, nor is it unique to India, but it has perhaps never been so knowingly emphasized as in the Theory of Rasa, and it is upon this aspect that the art of India asks us to look (with reference especially to music) and to the understanding of which we must give our attention.

Based on a text by Geeta Satyadeva Mayor

16 'The Music Room', or 'Harmony in Green and Rose'

Oil painting by Whistler, United States of America. 1860

THE ROMANTIC SADNESS of nineteenth-century music is all too often hinted at in bad nineteenth-century pictures, so that the good painters of the great musical age have to be particularly cautious in their approach to a theme which may easily become cloying. Such is the indirectness here that Whistler hedged *The Music Room* about with two alternative titles: *The Morning Call* came first; and in later years, when the mood for musical allusions was upon him, *Harmony in Green and Rose*. Perhaps, indeed, for Whistler himself the essential musicality of the picture dawned only gradually; perhaps for him, as for us, the first impression was of a pale morning sunshine, filtering in through the tall windows of a London house.

Whistler was born at Lowell, Massachusetts, but spent part of his boyhood in St. Petersburg (Leningrad). In his native America he would have seen the seasons change from the hazy heat of a New England summer to what his younger compatriot, the writer Henry James, called 'the terrible deadly pure polar pink that shows behind American winter woods'. In Russia he would have known a winter climate not so different from that of his homeland, a summer climate lighter and paler, with those endless white nights that astonish visitors from the southern world. How different the light of northern France and southern England, and how beguiling to the American; Henry James noted it too – *vague and dim and pretty* were the words he found for it. But it was Whistler, as has often been said, who invented the beauty of London fog; and it was he who chose musical analogies to describe his impressions of it – 'nocturnes', 'symphonies' and 'variations'.

In *The Music Room* the mist is only implied, not yet all-pervasive. We are in 1860; and Whistler, aged twenty-six, has only lately reached London, by way of Paris. The scene is laid in the house of his sister, the wife of Seymour Haden, a celebrated London surgeon and amateur artist of considerable distinction. The centre of the stage is occupied by the slender figure of a young woman in a black riding habit; she is Miss Boott, an American relative. Behind her, in the corner by the window, is Annie Haden, reading *Punch*. She has already posed for her uncle, a year since, in *At the Piano* – where she is seen in the curve of the long instrument, resting her arms on the lid and watching her mother at the keyboard. In that picture Mrs. Haden is in full view; here she is only glimpsed in the mirror, seated at an invisible piano. But we can guess from her expression that she is playing, and can almost imagine what the music is – Schubert, Chopin or Schumann, most likely – she would be sitting more upright for Beethoven, one suspects. Annie is apparently unconcerned by her mother's music; but Miss Boott is listening intently, and resting her left hand the while on an unexplained fall of chintz, patterned with flowers and leaves and birds, like the chintz of the window curtains.

This curious allusive indirectness may surprise us in an artist who afterwards courted publicity and exulted in scandal: possibly such exhibitionism was an over-compensating attempt to subdue that celebrated New England shyness and remoteness; possibly his true sensibility is better expressed in this masterpiece of indirect speech. At all events, we are reminded again of Henry James; and of another New Englander, the poet Emily Dickinson, who (we are told) preferred to sit out of sight in the shady hall while her friend played Haydn and Scarlatti in the long white drawing-room at Amherst.

Be that as it may, this 'mirror music' is marvellously caught and fixed in the young Whistler's evocation of the cultivated milieu of North Americans in Europe one hundred years ago. The 'vague dim pretty London light' crosses the summer trees in Cadogan Place; falls upon Annie's white muslin; just touches the dark cloth of Miss Boott's riding habit; gleams on the chintz and

James Macneill Whistler, American painter, was born at Lowell, Massachusetts, 1834, studied in Paris and from 1860 worked mainly in England. Among the French artists with whom he came into contact, Degas (see Plate 17), possibly influenced him most; and like many of the Impressionists of his time he was inspired also by the example of the Japanese colour prints which were introduced to Europe in the middle of the century. Whistler was more of an aesthete than his French contemporaries and developed a style in which his sensitivity to pattern and tonal harmony is displayed. Later in his life he gave to his paintings such musical terms as 'Variations', 'Harmonies' or 'Nocturnes' (views of London and the Thames at night).

16. 'THE MUSIC ROOM' or 'Harmony in Green and Rose' — Whistler. 1860.
Freer Gallery of Art, Washington, USA — Oil painting. 37½ x 28 in.: 95 x 71 cm.

the porcelain vase on the shelf under the looking-glass; glances off the opaline glass lampshade and the picture frames; and suffuses the pale face of Mrs. Haden at her hidden piano. On these waves of mild spring sunshine the music is mysteriously borne back to us, as though reflected in the mirror; and the room is full of those unheard melodies which a romantic poet found sweeter than melodies heard.

Roger Hinks †

Bibliography

J. Laver
Whistler
Faber, London, 1930

17 Degas' father listening to the guitarist Pagans

Oil painting by Degas, France. 1868–1869

THIS DOUBLE PORTRAIT represents the Spanish guitarist Pagans, well-known in his time, playing upon his guitar, and next to him, listening, Degas' father. The painting is a study in human contrast. The Spaniard is in the prime of his life, with full-blooded face, straight and vigorous body. One feels that he confronts the world as he sings, used to applause and conquest. The old man next to him is withdrawn within himself. Frail in body, he leans forward, his hands clasped over his knees. His hair and moustache are white, while that of the younger man is dark, abundant and strong.

As important as this contrast, however, is surely the manner in which the two men are welded together into a single group. The guitar is not only the centre of the picture; it also connects the two figures, who are entirely dependent upon one another. Were the right half of the painting lost, we would hardly be aware that the young man is actually playing and singing.

It is the absorbed expression of the old man who listens that makes us conscious of the music. The two figures are held together by the music, for it is the music that helps the forms to convey the inner relationship of things. Degas has brought out this contrast between the young man playing on his guitar and singing and the old man listening with complete lack of drama, in tones of grey, black, white and brown, a scheme of colour he frequently used. In the background appears an open piano upon which a book of music rests, providing Degas with a patch of white which acts as a foil to the face of the old man, and counterbalances the gentle forward inclination of his head and shoulders.

Degas was certainly aware that the introduction of the guitar as the musical instrument would bring to our minds a certain image: each instrument possesses its own character and associations; and the introduction of a harp, or a piano or a violin, for instance, would call forth a quite different picture. The guitar helps to bring out still more the contrast between age and youth, for we associate it with warm evenings in Spain or the Mediterranean, with gay songs and dances in the open; and indeed, it must have had this association for Degas too for he had often visited Naples as a child.

Degas has painted the faces in a clear light, and with infinite subtlety. He only painted portraits of those near to him, of his family and friends, and never for an order; and in this portrait of his father we sense the intimate knowledge Degas had of every line in the well-known face, and of the attitude and expression equally familiar to the son. His portraits formed the essential part of his work at the beginning of his career; and in this comparatively early work he paints his father with great tenderness. The artist is still a young man and has not become embittered by the blindness, ill-health and loneliness of his later life.

Degas has captured for ever a scene that must have been very familiar to him: we know that his father used to hold musical evenings on Mondays at his house in Paris, to which musicians and artists (including Degas' great contemporary Manet and his wife) used to come. Degas himself would interpret popular Neapolitan music which he knew as a child. This European tradition of musical evenings at home has been painted innumerable times, and is part of their tradition that Europeans appear to be losing. During those gas-lit evenings, among familiar faces and familiar objects, how often did the observant eyes of the artist watch his father's face and register that inward expression? How many times did he see his father withdrawn into his own world, a world made up in his own mind with all the feeling that his sensitive face tells us he was capable of?

Edgar Degas (1834–1917), French painter, one of the Impressionist group of painters, the new artistic movement which originated in Paris in the 1860's. The Impressionists introduced both a new subject matter and a new technique. They were concerned with the recording of the human scene of their times without comment. They sought to capture the immediate impression of the ordinary everyday scene and action – 'to capture the particular notation of the moment, in a word, the impression'. Whether the artist (like Monet, Pissarro and Sisley) concentrated more on landscape, or (like Manet, Renoir and Degas) more on the human figure, the intention and the technique was the same. In the first case the concern was with the authentic and living record of the contemporary environment; in the other, it was the recording of the contemporary everyday scene or action, but which could never be separated from the environment. Degas was the one among the Impressionists who more exclusively was concerned with the recording of the everyday actions of the people around him.

See also note to Plate 19, in *War and Peace*, vol. 1 of *Man through his Art*.

17. DEGAS' FATHER LISTENING TO THE GUITARIST PAGANS — Degas. 1868-9.
Museum of Fine Arts, Boston, USA — Oil painting. 31½ x 25 in.: 80 x 63 cm.

Tagore once said: 'Those of the audience who are appreciative are content to perfect the song in their own minds by the force of their feeling'. This indeed is what Degas' father is doing. The title of the picture tells us that Degas has noted the experience of listening; and how deeply he has observed that experience, and how sympathetically conveyed it to us in this painting. It is, indeed, this significant aspect of music, the human experience of listening, that Degas, once he has observed it, makes the real theme of this painting. The guitarist, so vividly portrayed too, is essential only as the one who produces the music, and to provide the living contrast between the young man and the old man, full of his 'dreamy load', immersed in the music and his thoughts. If there is a greater vigour in the younger man, it is the supreme expression of human experience on the face of the older man that is the pivot of the composition. Hence, the quiet placing of the area of white behind the head of the older man. If the Indian Ragamala painting on Plate 15 interprets the emotion that the tune evokes in the listener, Degas' painting brings before us the very act of listening.

Nothing perhaps could help more towards a better understanding of both Degas' painting and the Ragamala painting than a comparison of the two conceptions. The Indian miniature, it was said, interprets the emotion, or *rasa*, produced in the listener. Degas' painting shows us not the *rasa* itself, but the *rasika*, the one who 'tastes' *rasa*, who is sensitive enough to experience *rasa*. Degas has portrayed his father experiencing *rasa*. To the Indian mind aesthetic experience is an 'inscrutable spiritual activity, that is ever present and potentially realisable'. Something of this experience is expressed also in Whistler's painting (Plate 16), in which the young woman who has just returned from her ride is held momentarily immobile by the music she hears as she enters the room.

Anil de Silva

Bibliography

John Rewald
History of Impressionism
Museum of Modern Art, New York, 1961

J. B. Manson
The Life and Work of Edgar Degas
The Studio Ltd., London, 1927

18 African Harp

Mangbetu harp, Uele Valley, Congo. 19th century

THERE IS an obvious difference between the object represented here and all the other works reproduced in this album. Whereas the latter were created as images of what music is or how it affects man, the harp shown here is an instrument that produces music; one might say it is a utensil and not a work of art, and the man who made it, not an artist but a craftsman, who knew all the practical skills needed to make an excellent harp. In the present case, however, this distinction misses something essential: for this harp is not only visually satisfying as an instrument perfectly adapted to its intended use, but its form seems to anticipate the music it will produce.

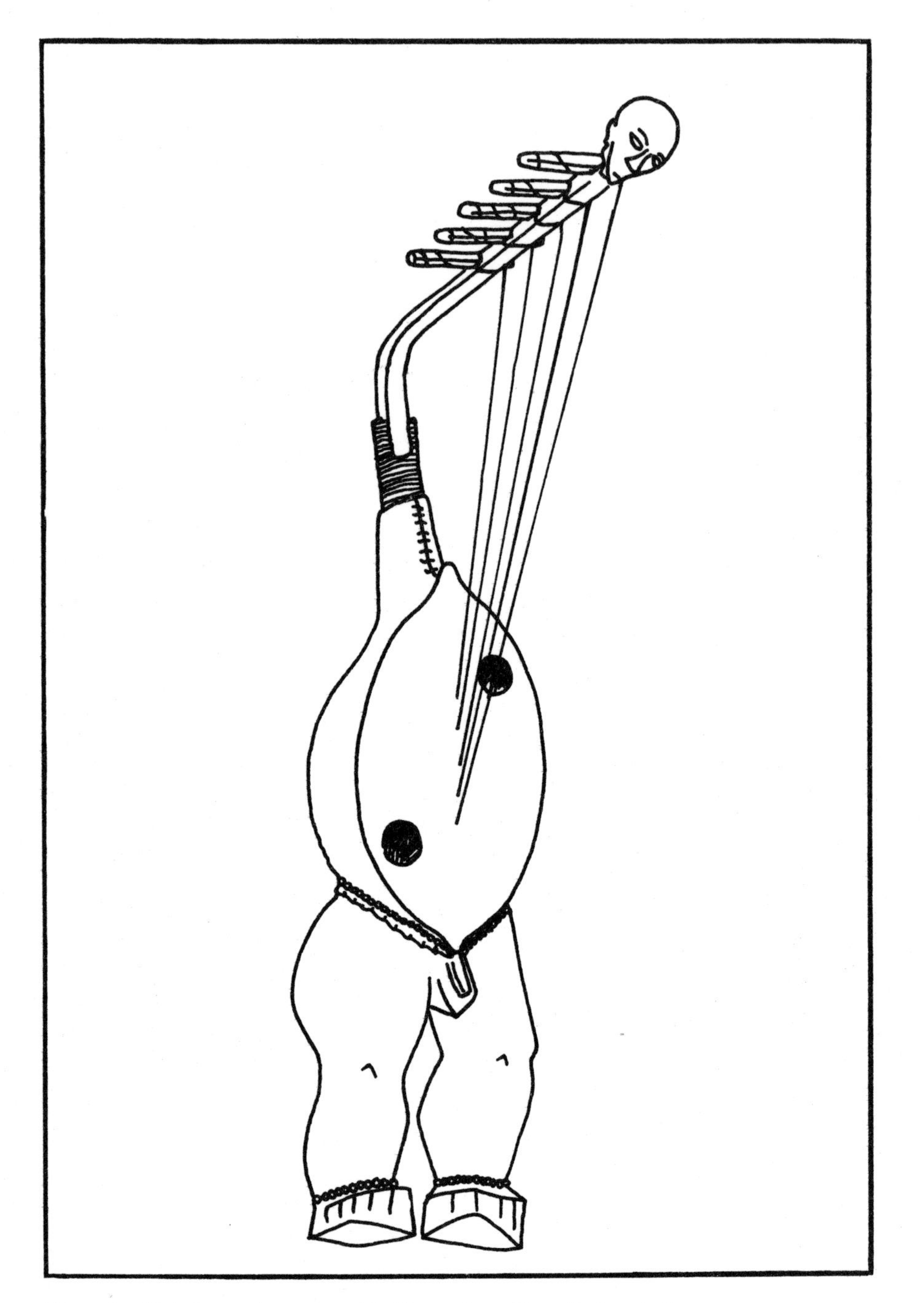

Fig. 18a. *Ngbaka anthropomorphic Harp, from Haut Oubangi, Congo.*

This form of harp in which the plastic qualities of an original art are combined with the technical requirements of the instrument is found only in the Northern Congo among a population originally from the Sudan (the Zandë, Mangbetu, Momvu, Bangba, Nzakara, Ngbandi, Ngbaka), and in the district to the west of the river, in the Gabonese forest and to the Atlantic littoral. Different tribes vary the style of these harp-statues, but only the Mangbetu carve their heads with these elongated craniums with tall headdress, in the image of their own heads which are formed in this way from childhood by a circular band. This elegant form is further prolonged by the chignon of false hair and basket-work worn at the back of the head. Among other tribes, like the Zandë, the head is rounder and the face flatter, and the headdress modified. Among the Ngbaka, as we see in Fig. 18a, the body is more complete.

The curved anthropomorphic harp is a very ancient instrument, and it figures in Egyptian painted funeral steles of the Second Theban Empire. There is not, however, necessarily any direct connection between the Egyptian harp and those found in the Northern Congo.

J.D.

18. AFRICAN HARP
The Reitberg Museum, Zurich

From the Uele Valley, Congo. 19th century.

This harp belongs to a group that scholars call 'harp-statues' or 'anthropomorphic harps'. These expressions are intended to indicate that the instruments are related in form to the human being, and more significantly, that they are strangely attuned not only to the physical appearance but also to the mood and spirit of the musicians who use them. The present harp is certainly not a naturalistic representation of the human form, and only in a very general way are we able to distinguish the forms – apart from the beautifully carved head – and there are no recognisable arms or legs. Some harps of this group, however, do display the anthropomorphic image complete, and in these the resonance box is frankly the body and terminates in two thick legs which serve as a solid support for the whole (Fig. 18a).

This 'harp-statue' comes from the Mangbetu tribe in the valley of the Uele in Northern Congo, and possesses that remarkable plastic harmony expected of the Mangbetu and their neighbours the Zandë, whose aristocratic civilisation attached so much social importance to aesthetic values. Particularly striking is the carving of the fine, elongated head, with its almond eyes, its long thin mouth in relief and its delicate chin, and the elegant curve of the swan-like neck. The graceful form of the neck and head is opposed to the rather rigorous geometry of the resonance box. The wooden resonance box

Fig. 18b. *Three Poets with their Harps. Drawing by an explorer.* 1871.

is covered in skin tightly stretched and stitched to the edges. The face of the box is pierced by two round holes, disposed diagonally, which serve to modify the sound. The five strings, made of vegetable fibre, are fixed to wooden keys terminating in circles.

We must visualise the body of the harp resting on the knees of the minstrel as he plays, its body pressed against his, the player's left hand strumming the cords while his right hand holds the upper part with its keys as he sings. The instrument then becomes his companion, his second self, not only in the musical sense, but also in the visual and symbolic sense. Its shape follows the shape of his body, and the head reflects the attitude of the singer. In short, the harp embodies something of the human chant itself, and in doing so it does not sacrifice its functional perfection. This harp is indeed a work of art, inasmuch as the essence of any work of art, as defined by a great modern painter, is its ability to 'render visible'.

Four principal roles in the Mangbetu and Zandë society were those of the sorcerer, diviner, guardian of the oracles, and poet. The harp, the instrument of the poet, was inseparable from the songs and ballads of this society. These songs and ballads – of praise, of legend, and of social satire – played the double role of music and oral theatre. On occasion, when inspiration failed the singer, the harp was played alone. The poet was always a man. He was first a musician, and would become a master only when he proved his proficiency as a singer, that is, his ability to improvise while accompanying his harp of five strings (Fig. 18b, drawn by an explorer in 1871, shows us three poets with their harps). These poets lived by their talent, sometimes attaching themselves to the Court, sometimes travelling from village to village. Eric Dampierre, in *Poètes Nzakara*, tells of two European explorers, who, in the nineteenth century, were the first to penetrate into the Zande country, and were astonished at the quality of emotion of these songs. 'The poets possessed an instinctive love of their art. Passionately fond of music, they got from their instruments sounds which moved them to the most profound depths of their beings. The concerts that they gave for each other were extraordinary . . . a poet would play his harp during twenty-four hours without leaving it for a second, forgetting to eat or drink . . . I have frequently seen friends arm in arm keeping time to a measure with a movement of their heads, plunged together into a state of ecstasy . . .'. The poets held a high opinion of themselves, the account continues, and from the first song they showed that they were a group apart:

'If you have no use for me, go.
Do you possess the food of life
That one eats so that one does not die?
I do not like these attitudes.
I am a musician!
Woman who does nothing but laugh,
Woman with dusty hair,
I do not like these attitudes.
I am a musician!'

Jacqueline Delange

Bibliography

Eric Dampierre (ed.)
Poètes Nzakara
Classiques Africains, Julliard, Paris, 1963

19. 'AROUND HER'
Musée d'Art Moderne, Paris

Chagall. Signed and dated in 1945.
Oil painting. $51\frac{1}{4}$ x $42\frac{3}{4}$ in.: 131 x 109 cm.

'Around Her' 19

Oil painting by Marc Chagall, Russia. 1938–1945

Marc Chagall was born in 1887 at Vitebsk in Russia. He belonged to the Jewish Hassadist sect which emphasized the omnipresence of God, the importance of prayer and the possibility of miracles.

He seems conscious of the double character of East and West in himself, and in 1913 painted the 'Self Portrait with Seven Fingers' (now in the Municipal Museum, Amsterdam). In this painting Hebrew characters form the background, and on the right the little Russian town appears like a vision, and the dreaming cow; and the Eiffel Tower introduces the West. The principal elements of the painter's personality already appear in this painting. Chagall, however, denies any symbolic meaning, and insists that he paints as he sees human beings and objects, green rabbis, blue angels!

He was one of nine children, and his family inspired some of his first drawings: his famous picture 'The Green Violinist' (now in the Guggenheim Museum, New York) was inspired by his uncle who used to play the violin. Chagall reveals a pure vision of a unique world entirely created out of memory. His reality was always a blend of the past and present. In 1909 he studied under Leon Bakst. In 1910 he visited Paris, returning to Russia just before the first World War. After the Revolution he was appointed Commissar for Fine Arts for the district of Vitebsk, and also worked for the Yiddish Theatre in Moscow painting murals and designing decors and costumes. In 1922 he returned to France, and in 1941 he went to the United States invited by the Museum of Modern Art. He now again lives in France.

L.L.

'I WILL BE A MUSICIAN', Chagall used to say in his childhood, and although in this painting, 'Around Her', we cannot see any of those musicians so dear to him, there are certainly very few pictures wrapped in such a musical atmosphere. The depth of the blue, the lightness of the blue-white bodies flying in the air, the luminous crescent moon, all have an exceptional melodic resonance. Even if he had not said so himself, we would guess that he likes to paint while listening to music.

This painting was started in 1938 when he was already caught up in the anguish of racial persecution and the forebodings of the destructions to follow during the second World War. In the foreground the beloved weeps, while the vision of a married couple amidst the dark leaves of a tree symbolises the happiness of love. The bird and its candle throw out a feeble light; and the head of a painter put in upside down produces a dramatic effect; to the left, on the canvas on the easel, a cow dreams.

In the middle distance, enclosed in a large clear circle, which isolates it from the menacing and sombre reality, is a village bathed in moonlight, while an angel descending from the sky protects this vision which is filled with a sense of peace and serenity.

This village, 'sad and gay', its houses with open doors and windows – a detail that psychologists tell us reveals the happy and free childhood of the painter – is the town of his Russian childhood, Vitebsk, with its 'blue stars and violet earth . . . ; its noisy gossips sitting outdoors . . . ; on market days, when the peasants and cats were alive in unbelievable confusion', as Chagall describes the town to us. 'The sparkling colours revealed in the sky; the sabbatical dinner with its white candles; the Passover, with its red wine in full glasses, the wine reflecting a dark, royal lilac; the ghetto, designed for the Jewish people; and the heat of the Arabian desert crossed (by the Jewish people) with such anguish . . .', and 'the house of my grandfather, a butcher, who ritually killed the cows and sheep, the house full of suspended skins drying like linen . . .'. In this house an uncle used to play the violin while the child and grandfather listened. When, in his autobiography, Chagall recalls this uncle with his violin, it is Rembrandt he brings to mind; again making one the two arts so dear to him. It was in this Jewish atmosphere that Chagall grew up.

In 1907, in St. Petersburg, he met Bella. It was love at first sight, and his paintings became a love-song for her who became his wife. He dedicated 'Around Her' to Bella. Meanwhile, in the miserable room he dreams: 'suddenly the ceiling opens and a winged being descends, resplendent, filling the room with movement and clouds and the rush of wings. I think, an angel! I cannot open my eyes; everything is too light, too radiant'. He glances about, ascends and is transported past the ceiling of his room taking with him 'all the light and the blue air'.

We see the reason now for the candles, the angel, the blue air, the little cow, and the beloved. These are the significant motifs in the painting, and their introduction and development can be followed through the time of his early life in Russia. There he stayed, until his teacher, Bakst, paid him the unusual compliment: 'Now your colours sing!'. From the beginning Bakst noticed this musical tendency, which is so evident in 'Around Her', a tendency which the early nineteenth-century French painter Delacroix called 'characteristic of a masterpiece'. In 1910 Chagall arrived in Paris, and from that moment his canvases reveal the influence of Paris and the importance he was henceforth to attach to a well constructed composition. But however great was this influence in the formation of his painting, Chagall knew how to 'keep his roots', as he would say. He remains always in some way a Russian Jew. He brought with him to France his own riches: an oriental logic and human warmth, a pantheistic love for all creatures, a love that he extends to man-made objects; and above all a global vision, that oriental attitude that seeks to assemble everything in unity rather than to divide and classify. The spirit of synthesis in Chagall embraces with this same ardent love all that is art without dividing it into its various categories of music, painting and poetry.

The importance of Chagall lies not only in the remarkable emotive power of his art, but above all in the balance he attained within himself between the two cultures. He is the meeting of East and West. Perhaps more significant than the oriental sense of unity that he possesses, is his interest in the strong construction of a painting as evolved in the West. When questioned about the symbolic meaning of the animals, trees, houses and other objects in his paintings, he insisted that, 'more than the meaning of these elements, I would like to emphasize their constructive character in my painting'. And elsewhere he explains why he separated a head from the body of one of his figures: 'I needed an empty space just at that place'. And when he places the painter's head upside down in this painting, is it to balance the picture or is it some obscure symbolism? We appreciate how profoundly the different arts are associated and combined in his mind, when before his painting we witness how, to serve the plastic demands of his art, he calls forth the most poetical or musical elements.

His paintings are a projection of his inner world, in which painting, poetry and music merge into one. No-one, probably, has deserved as much as Chagall the definition he himself gave of Rembrandt, that 'he lived his paintings as a great biblical ancestor'.

Lilian Lassen

Bibliography

Marc Chagall
Ma vie
Stock, Paris, 1957

20. 'THE MUSICIANS'
Private Collection

de Staël. 1952.
Oil painting. $63\frac{3}{4}$ x 45 in.: 162 x 114 cm.

'The Musicians' 20

Oil painting by Nicolas de Staël, France. 1952

Nicolas de Staël was born in 1914 at St. Petersburg, Russia, and died in 1955 at Antibes in the South of France. At the time of the Revolution his family left Russia for Brussels, where, from 1932–33 he studied at the Académie des Beaux-Arts. Subsequently he travelled to Holland, where he became acquainted with Rembrandt's painting; and to Paris, where it seems he was particularly inspired by those painters who gave so much importance to pure colour. Among these painters were such artists as Matisse and Braque, representatives of the Fauves movement of the early years of the twentieth-century, who continued in their painting to stress the importance of pure colour. Nicolas de Staël developed an original and powerful style of painting which relied on simplicity and strength of design employing large areas of a few pure and vivid colours. Certainly his near-abstract painting which sought to capture and vividly record the essence of the scene or event, was of influence on the pure abstract painters who were to follow him.

THERE IS an ancient legend that begins, 'Once upon a time, there was a hen that laid golden eggs . . .'. Nicolas de Staël, in this painting, brings forth golden melodies, powerful and sonorous. The room is full of this golden sound that sings, dances and echoes everywhere, filling the space with a brilliant splendour, the whole universe seemingly inundated by a golden sound.

It sings of love, in a high key, in the red of the air; it breathes memories of love in the yellow of the light; and laments the sadness of love in the blue of the shadows.

Whence does this passionate dance of love spring? From the clarinet, or the trumpet? No, it is not the instruments that create this sonorous dance; it is born of the very existence of the musicians – the music is produced by their whole being, their eyes, their hands, their bodies, their feet, before finally emerging from the tube of the flute to create and fill the pictorial space. Lightly or heavily, high-pitched or bass, this golden sound that never ceases transmits the love, sadness, joy and fears of all men, as if this golden melody were the respiration of all human beings.

To bring this out in a painting it is not necessary to have a complicated theory or extreme virtuosity of craftsmanship. What is essential is to possess a purity of sentiment – as pure as transparent water – the power to perceive and experience that transcends the externals of things, of life and matter, and discovers their original essence and rhythm. Nicolas de Staël understands well this mystery of life and matter, and demonstrates it by the brilliance of his palette, in which each colour – each sound created – flows like a human movement, and time of life becomes in his canvas space of life.

This called for rich primary colours. The Fauves at the beginning of the century tried to translate human passion by the vehement contrast of bright colours, with which they represented the whole world. In the same manner, this sonorous painting has an absolute confidence in the purity and saturation of its colours. By the three colours, red, yellow and blue, de Staël expresses wonderfully an optimism and *joie de vivre*. The colours, new and fresh, which are in reality nothing else but the enchanted sound of the flute, the clarinet and the trumpet, create a free movement, flowing everywhere, singing a melody never sung before. In this burst of colour and light, it is the red and yellow that play the principal role. They clash, animate the atmosphere, and finally create a harmony charged with an almost cosmic power, as if they were the supreme expression of a universal energy.

As the sound reaches its ascendency the colour reaches its fulness. In this simple composition, the musicians become de-materialised, weightless, giving place to a world of music. In fact, it is not the men, the musicians, that the painter wishes to represent on his canvas; there is, in reality, only space, a space filled with music, a space which exists only through the music.

A musician is a being who exists by the sound he creates. All the painter then must express is this 'existence in sound'. It is first the sound he creates, and then follows in this very sound the man, and one is conscious that the man exists only by virtue of the sound, and thus by virtue of the sonorous colours that de Staël has made live on his canvas – his red, his yellow, his blue – and above all the juxtaposition of these colours one with another. The pattern of this juxtaposition of colours is not in the least complicated, but on the contrary very simple like that of the Fauves, and it is precisely in this simplicity that the painter has achieved that intensity. It is to this intensity and powerful simplicity that the painting owes its strength, which pierces direct to the heart of contemporary music.

The music we hear is not that of Mozart or Beethoven, but it is the rhythm and melody which surround us in our lives. Powerful and rich, it stirs us and encourages us in the pursuit of our own everyday lives. This is the message that de Staël wishes to communicate to us through this powerful and strong and beautiful composition.

Soichi Tominaga

Bibliography

Douglas Cooper
Nicolas de Staël
Masters and Movements
Weidenfeld & Nicolson, 1961